JAMESTOWN  EDUCATION

TIMED READINGS

Third Edition

Fifty 400-Word Passages
with Questions for
Building Reading Speed

BOOK ONE

Edward Spargo

 **Glencoe
McGraw-Hill**

New York, New York   Columbus, Ohio   Chicago, Illinois   Peoria, Illinois   Woodland Hills, California

JAMESTOWN EDUCATION

Titles in This Series
Timed Readings, Third Edition
Timed Readings in Literature
Timed Readings Plus

Glencoe/McGraw-Hill

A Division of The McGraw-Hill Companies

Timed Readings, Third Edition
Book One

Cover and text design: Deborah Hulsey Christie

ISBN: 0-89061-503-9

Send all queries:
Glencoe/McGraw-Hill
8787 Orion Place
Columbus, OH 43240-4027

Manufactured in the United States of America.

18 19 20 21 22 021 10 09 08 07

Contents

Introduction to the Student

These *Timed Readings* are designed to help you become a faster and better reader. As you progress through the book, you will find yourself growing in reading speed and comprehension. You will be challenged to increase your reading rate while maintaining a high level of comprehension.

Reading, like most things, improves with practice. If you practice improving your reading speed, you will improve. As you will see, the rewards of improved reading speed will be well worth your time and effort.

Why Read Faster?

The quick and simple answer is that faster readers are better readers. Does this statement surprise you? You might think that fast readers would miss something and their comprehension might suffer. This is not true, for two reasons:

1. Faster readers comprehend faster. When you read faster, the writer's message is coming to you faster and makes sense sooner. Ideas are interconnected. The writer's thoughts are all tied together, each one leading to the next. The more quickly you can see how ideas are related to each other, the more quickly you can comprehend the meaning of what you are reading.

2. Faster readers concentrate better. Concentration is essential for comprehension. If your mind is wandering you can't understand what you are reading. A lack of concentration causes you to re-read, sometimes over and over, in order to comprehend. Faster readers concentrate better because there's less time for distractions to interfere. Comprehension, in turn, contributes to concentration. If you are concentrating and comprehending, you will not become distracted.

Want to Read More?

Do you wish that you could read more? (or, at least, would you like to do your required reading in less time?) Faster reading will help.

The illustration on the next page shows the number of books someone might read over a period of ten years. Let's see what faster reading could do for you. Look at the stack of books read by a slow reader and the stack

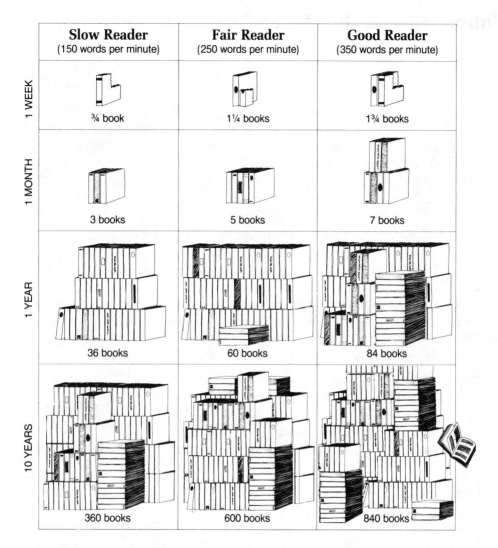

	Slow Reader (150 words per minute)	Fair Reader (250 words per minute)	Good Reader (350 words per minute)
1 WEEK	¾ book	1¼ books	1¾ books
1 MONTH	3 books	5 books	7 books
1 YEAR	36 books	60 books	84 books
10 YEARS	360 books	600 books	840 books

read by a good reader. (We show a speed of 350 words a minute for our "good" reader, but many fast readers can more than double that speed.) Let's say, however, that you are now reading at a rate of 150 words a minute. The illustration shows you reading 36 books a year. By increasing your reading speed to 250 words a minute, you could increase the number of books to 60 a year.

We have arrived at these numbers by assuming that the readers in our illustration read for one hour a day, six days a week, and that an average book is about 72,000 words long. Many people do not read that much, but they might if they could learn to read better and faster.

Faster reading doesn't *take* time, it *saves* time!

How to Use This Book

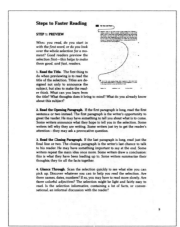

1 Learn the Four Steps
Study and learn the four steps to follow to become a better and faster reader. The steps are covered on pages 9, 10, 11, and 12.

2 Preview
Turn to the selection you are going to read and wait for the instructor's signal to preview. Your instructor will allow 30 seconds for previewing.

3 Begin reading
When your instructor gives you the signal, begin reading. Read at a slightly faster-than-normal speed. Read well enough so that you will be able to answer questions about what you have read.

7 Fill in the progress graph
Enter your score and plot your reading time on the graph on page 118 or 119. The right-hand side of the graph shows your words-per-minute reading speed. Write this number at the bottom of the page on the line labeled *Words per Minute.*

4 Record your time When you finish reading, look at the blackboard and note your reading time. Your reading time will be the lowest time remaining on the board, or the next number to be erased. Write this time at the bottom of the page on the line labeled *Reading Time*.

5 Answer the questions Answer the ten questions on the next page. There are five fact questions and five thought questions. Pick the *best* answer to each question and put an x in the box beside it.

6 Correct your answers Using the Answer Key on pages 116 and 117, correct your work. Circle your wrong answers and put an x in the box you should have marked. Score 10 points for each correct answer. Write your score at the bottom of the page on the line labeled *Comprehension Score*.

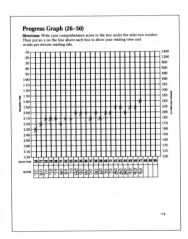

Progress Graph (26–50)
Directions: Write your comprehension score in the box under the selection number. Then put an x on the line above each box to show your reading time and words-per-minute reading rate.

Instructions for the Pacing Drills

From time to time your instructor may wish to conduct pacing drills using *Timed Readings*. For this work you need to use the Pacing Dots printed in the margins of your book pages. The dots will help you regulate your reading speed to match the pace set by your instructor or announced on the reading cassette tape.

Pacing Dots

You will be reading at the correct pace if you are at the dot when your instructor says "Mark" or when you hear a tone on the tape. If you are ahead of the pace, read a little more slowly; if you are behind the pace, increase your reading speed. Try to match the pace exactly.

Follow these steps.

Step 1: Record the pace. At the bottom of the page, write on the line labeled *Words per Minute* the rate announced by the instructor or by the speaker on the tape.

Step 2: Begin reading. Wait for the signal to begin reading. Read at a slightly faster-than-normal speed. You will not know how on-target your pace is until you hear your instructor say "Mark" or until you hear the first tone on the tape. After a little practice you will be able to select an appropriate starting speed most of the time.

Step 3: Adjust your pace. As you read, try to match the pace set by the instructor or the tape. Read more slowly or more quickly as necessary. You should be reading the line beside the dot when you hear the pacing signal. The pacing sounds may distract you at first. Don't worry about it. Keep reading and your concentration will return.

Step 4: Stop and answer questions. Stop reading when you are told to, even if you have not finished the selection. Answer the questions right away. Correct your work and record your score on the line *Comprehension Score*. Strive to maintain 80 percent comprehension on each drill as you gradually increase your pace.

Step 5: Fill in the pacing graph. Transfer your words-per-minute rate to the box labeled *Pace* on the pacing graph on page 120. Then plot your comprehension score on the line above the box.

These pacing drills are designed to help you become a more flexible reader. They encourage you to "break out" of a pattern of reading everything at the same speed.

The drills help in other ways, too. Sometimes in a reading program you reach a certain level and bog down. You don't seem able to move on and progress. The pacing drills will help you to work your way out of such slumps and get your reading program moving again.

Steps to Faster Reading

STEP 1: PREVIEW

When you read, do you start in with the first word, or do you look over the whole selection for a moment? Good readers preview the selection first—this helps to make them good, and fast, readers.

1. Read the Title. The first thing to do when previewing is to read the title of the selection. Titles are designed not only to announce the subject, but also to make the reader think. What can you learn from the title? What thoughts does it bring to mind? What do you already know about this subject?

2. Read the Opening Paragraph. If the first paragraph is long, read the first sentence or two instead. The first paragraph is the writer's opportunity to greet the reader. He may have something to tell you about what is to come. Some writers announce what they hope to tell you in the selection. Some writers tell why they are writing. Some writers just try to get the reader's attention—they may ask a provocative question.

3. Read the Closing Paragraph. If the last paragraph is long, read just the final line or two. The closing paragraph is the writer's last chance to talk to his reader. He may have something important to say at the end. Some writers repeat the main idea once more. Some writers draw a conclusion: this is what they have been leading up to. Some writers summarize their thoughts; they tie all the facts together.

4. Glance Through. Scan the selection quickly to see what else you can pick up. Discover whatever you can to help you read the selection. Are there names, dates, numbers? If so, you may have to read more slowly. Are there colorful adjectives? The selection might be light and fairly easy to read. Is the selection informative, containing a lot of facts, or conversational, an informal discussion with the reader?

---

22 By Sun and Stars

Migratory birds do not travel as fast as some people once believed. A German scientist in 1895, for example, attributed speeds in excess of 200 miles an hour to some birds during migration. Research later showed that this estimate was much too high. The peregrine falcon flies 165 to 180 miles per hour while chasing food, but very few birds can fly this fast. Birds have two speeds. One is for normal flying, and a faster one is for escaping enemies or chasing food. Most songbirds have cruising speeds between 25 and 50 miles per hour during migration.

One of the most amazing things about migration is that some birds raised without adult guidance or experience in actual migration can orient to the proper direction across vast stretches of water.

Reading Time _____ Comprehension Score _____ Words per Minute _____ 57

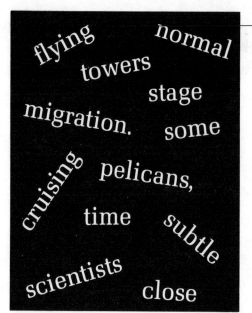

STEP 2: READ FOR MEANING

When you read, do you just see words? Are you so occupied reading words that you sometimes fail to get the meaning? Good readers see beyond the words—they read for meaning. This makes them faster readers.

1. Build Concentration. You cannot read with understanding if you are not concentrating. Every reader's mind wanders occasionally; it is not a cause for alarm. When you discover that your thoughts have strayed, correct the situation right away. The longer you wait, the harder it becomes. Avoid distractions and distracting situations. Outside noises and activities will compete for your attention if you let them. Keep the preview information in mind as you read. This will help to focus your attention on the selection.

2. Read in Thought Groups. Individual words do not tell us much. They must be combined with other words in order to yield meaning. To obtain meaning from the printed page, therefore, the reader should see the words in meaningful combinations. If you see only a word at a time (called word-by-word reading), your comprehension suffers along with your speed. To improve both speed and comprehension, try to group the words into phrases which have a natural relationship to each other. For practice, you might want to read aloud, trying to speak the words in meaningful combinations.

3. Question the Author. To sustain the pace you have set for yourself, and to maintain a high level of comprehension, question the writer as you read. Continually ask yourself such questions as, "What does this mean? What is he saying now? How can I use this information?" Questions like these help you to concentrate fully on the selection.

Steps to Faster Reading

STEP 3: GRASP PARAGRAPH SENSE

The paragraph is the basic unit of meaning. If you can discover quickly and understand the main point of each paragraph, you can comprehend the author's message. Good readers know how to find the main ideas of paragraphs quickly. This helps to make them faster readers.

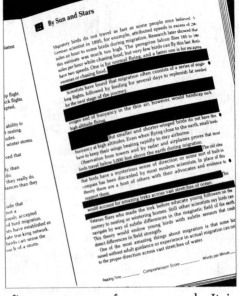

1. Find the Topic Sentence. The topic sentence, the sentence containing the main idea, is often the first sentence of a paragraph. It is followed by other sentences which support, develop, or explain the main idea. Sometimes a topic sentence comes at the end of a paragraph. When it does, the supporting details come first, building the base for the topic sentence. Some paragraphs do not have a topic sentence. Such paragraphs usually create a mood or feeling, rather than present information.

2. Understand Paragraph Structure. Every well-written paragraph has purpose. The purpose may be to inform, define, explain, persuade, compare or contrast, illustrate, and so on. The purpose should always relate to the main idea and expand on it. As you read each paragraph, see how the body of the paragraph is used to tell you more about the main idea or topic sentence. Read the supporting details intelligently, recognizing that what you are reading is all designed to develop the single main idea.

Steps to Faster Reading

STEP 4: ORGANIZE FACTS

When you read, do you tend to see a lot of facts without any apparent connection or relationship? Understanding how the facts all fit together to deliver the author's message is, after all, the reason for reading. Good readers organize facts as they read. This helps them to read rapidly and well.

1. Discover the Writer's Plan. Look for a clue or signal word early in the article which might reveal the author's structure. Every writer has a plan or outline which he follows. If the reader can discover his method of organization, he has the key to understanding the message. Sometimes the author gives you obvious signals. If he says, "There are three reasons . . ." the wise reader looks for a listing of the three items. Other less obvious signal words such as *moreover, otherwise, consequently* all tell the reader the direction the writer's message will take.

2. Relate as You Read. As you read the selection, keep the information learned during the preview in mind. See how the ideas you are reading all fit into place. Consciously strive to relate what you are reading to the title. See how the author is carrying through in his attempt to piece together a meaningful message. As you discover the relationship among the ideas, the message comes through quickly and clearly.

**Timed
Reading
Selections**

1   A Great Composer

Ludwig van Beethoven was one of the greatest composers who ever lived. He taught people that they could be freer when they wrote music. Before his time, music was composed for a special purpose. Often it was church music. Or, music was written to entertain at parties and dances. Beethoven did not think that music needed to have a practical use. He thought people should listen to music just for itself.

Beethoven was born in Germany in 1770. He was a very musical child. The boy learned to play the violin and the piano. But he was not happy at home. His mother died when he was in his teens. After that, his father was often drunk and bad-tempered. Beethoven became a tutor in a rich family. He was glad to get a job. His student's mother was very kind to the young teacher. She helped him meet many famous musicians. One of these was Mozart. Mozart heard the boy play the piano. He said, "That boy will give the world something worth listening to."

In a few years, Beethoven was ready to leave his teaching job. He went to the city of Vienna. There he wrote a lot of music. Some people who heard his music did not like it. They thought it was too loud and forceful. But soon most people came to admire his work.

When Beethoven was in his twenties, he began to go deaf. The deafness changed his behavior. He became withdrawn and moody. His friends found him hard to be around. But he kept composing even when he lost all his hearing. The music he heard was in his head.

Beethoven died when he was 57 years old. Most of his friends and family had deserted him. This had caused Beethoven a great deal of grief. But at least he had had his music. He had composed over a hundred pieces. His music spanned two stages of music history. His early music was more formal. It followed certain steps and patterns. But his later music changed. That style is now called romantic music. This type of music is written to stir the listener's feelings. Sometimes a piece tells a story. Beethoven learned to use music, not words, for the story. This romantic style changed the way people thought about music. Many later composers gained new ideas from Beethoven's musical discoveries.

Recalling Facts

1. Beethoven was born in
   - ☐ a. France.
   - ☐ b. Germany.
   - ☐ c. England.

2. The boy got a job as a
   - ☐ a. violinist.
   - ☐ b. singer.
   - ☐ c. tutor.

3. When Beethoven was in his twenties, he began to go
   - ☐ a. deaf.
   - ☐ b. blind.
   - ☐ c. crazy.

4. During his life, Beethoven composed
   - ☐ a. only a few pieces.
   - ☐ b. five hundred pieces.
   - ☐ c. over a hundred pieces.

5. Beethoven's later style is now called
   - ☐ a. baroque music.
   - ☐ b. romantic music.
   - ☐ c. country music.

Understanding the Passage

6. The young Beethoven
   - ☐ a. was very talented.
   - ☐ b. did not get along with his mother.
   - ☐ c. played the trumpet.

7. Beethoven's father
   - ☐ a. begged him not to leave home.
   - ☐ b. died when Beethoven was in his teens.
   - ☐ c. was not kind to his son.

8. Mozart apparently thought that Beethoven
   - ☐ a. had a bad temper.
   - ☐ b. should stop playing the piano.
   - ☐ c. would become famous.

9. Beethoven's deafness made him
   - ☐ a. stop writing music.
   - ☐ b. difficult to socialize with.
   - ☐ c. talk very loudly.

10. Beethoven's music
    - ☐ a. changed the way later composers thought.
    - ☐ b. is unimportant in today's music world.
    - ☐ c. ended the romantic era of music.

2 Picture This

Many events in our lives give us special memories. A camera helps to preserve those moments. Looking through photographs is a way to keep those times alive. To capture just the right look, it helps to know how to use a camera.

First you need the right kind of film for your camera type. Then you need to load the film. This should be done away from bright lights. Be careful not to open the camera until the film is finished and rewound. If this happens you risk exposure and loss of pictures.

You want to make sure the subject of your picture is centered. This is done by placing the subject in the center of your viewfinder. You may want to take a picture of more than one person. In that case, focus on the center of the group.

Light is a big factor in effective photos. When you are outside, it is best to keep the sun behind you. Pictures taken inside usually need a flash for good lighting. However, to get a muted look, you may wish to forget the flash. It is fun to experiment with light for new effects.

Some cameras come with a self-timer. This is especially helpful if you want to include yourself in the picture. At family gatherings it is nice to be part of the group shot. Center the photo with your position in mind. Press the timer button and get into place. About fifteen seconds will go by. The flash will go off.

Care of your camera is very important. You should avoid getting it wet. Never let your camera sit in a hot place. Do not take it apart yourself.

Each person has his or her own style of taking pictures. Some like taking pictures of people. Others look for an outdoor scene as their subject. Some photographers like shots to be posed. Others enjoy taking candids. This is when people do not know their picture is being taken.

Now you are ready to take your picture. Hold the camera steady, focus, and click! When the film is developed, you can see your results. Don't be upset if your first pictures are not as good as you had hoped. Good photography takes practice. Taking pictures is a full-time job for some people. You might think of working for a newspaper or magazine. Or you could just use your skill for your own reward.

Recalling Facts

1. When you load film into your camera,
   - ☑ a. the room should not be well-lit.
   - ☐ b. count how many pictures you have.
   - ☐ c. make sure the window is open.

2. If you open the camera before the film is finished,
   - ☐ a. take it out and have it developed.
   - ☑ b. you will lose pictures from exposure.
   - ☐ c. reload the film again.

3. When you take pictures outside, the sun should
   - ☐ a. shine in your face.
   - ☐ b. be behind you.
   - ☐ c. feel very hot.

4. You should not let a camera
   - ☐ a. be returned to the store.
   - ☐ b. get used by someone else.
   - ☐ c. get hot or wet.

5. Candids are pictures
   - ☐ a. which are not posed.
   - ☐ b. that come out fuzzy.
   - ☐ c. that are taken on vacation.

Understanding the Passage

6. A self-timer makes it possible
   - ☑ a. for you to be in the picture.
   - ☐ b. to take more than one picture at a time.
   - ☐ c. to take pictures underwater.

7. Cameras help us to remember
   - ☐ a. to center people in a picture.
   - ☑ b. special events.
   - ☐ c. to rewind the film.

8. Light can be experimented with
   - ☐ a. to create a different effect.
   - ☐ b. to block out your subject.
   - ☑ c. when you are all out of film.

9. Before using your camera, it is important to
   - ☑ a. have the right kind of film.
   - ☐ b. have your photo album ready.
   - ☐ c. tell people you are taking pictures.

10. A newspaper or magazine can
    - ☐ a. help you answer questions about your camera.
    - ☐ b. supply you with plenty of film.
    - ☑ c. offer a good job for a photographer.

The solar system is made of the sun and all the obje... it. The solar system is about 4 billion years old. The p... objects that circle the sun. There are nine planets. M... to the sun. Pluto is the farthest away. Some of the p... of rock and iron. The Earth is a rocky planet. But th... not Earth-like. Jupiter is one of these planets.

Jupiter is the largest planet in the solar system. Ancie... the planet after the king of the Roman gods. Jupiter ... planet to the sun. It lies between Mars and Saturn. At... measures about 89,000 miles. That makes it eleven tim... bigger than the Earth.

Like all the planets, Jupiter orbits around the sun. It takes 365 days for the Earth to complete one orbit. But it takes Jupiter almost twelve years to travel around the sun. Jupiter also rotates, or spins, just as the Earth does. On the Earth, one spin takes 24 hours. But Jupiter spins very fast. It only takes ten hours for Jupiter to complete its spin.

Jupiter's surface cannot be seen from Earth. Many layers of dense clouds hide the planet. But scientists have ideas about what its surface is like. They think that Jupiter is a fluid planet. That means that it is mostly made of gas and liquid. The clouds that surround Jupiter make light and dark stripes on the planet. One cloud is known as the Great Red Spot. This spot changes place from year to year. Scientists think that the spot may be an intense storm.

Jupiter's clouds are very cold. They may be as much as 236 degrees below zero. But underneath the clouds, the planet is very hot. The temperature can climb to 34,000 degrees. Some scientists say that life forms might be able to exist in Jupiter's clouds. But that has not been proven yet.

Jupiter has sixteen moons. Some of these moons are made of ice. Others seem to be made of rocks. Jupiter also has a thin ring around it. The planet Saturn is famous for rings like these.

Several spacecraft have flown past Jupiter. They have taken pictures of the planet. They have also tested its clouds. That is how they have discovered what they are made from. The spacecraft have helped scientists to learn more about Jupiter.

Recalling Facts

1. Mercury is the
   - ☐ a. closest planet to the sun.
   - ☐ b. coolest planet.
   - ☐ c. moon of Venus.

2. Ancient scientists named Jupiter after
   - ☐ a. a great general.
   - ☐ b. the king of the Roman gods.
   - ☐ c. someone's father.

3. Jupiter's surface is
   - ☐ a. easy to see.
   - ☐ b. invisible from the earth.
   - ☐ c. very rocky.

4. The Great Red Spot is probably a
   - ☐ a. moon.
   - ☐ b. fire.
   - ☐ c. storm.

5. Some of Jupiter's moons are made of
   - ☐ a. gold.
   - ☐ b. ice.
   - ☐ c. clouds.

Understanding the Passage

6. One day on Jupiter lasts
   - ☐ a. twenty hours.
   - ☐ b. twenty-four hours.
   - ☐ c. ten hours.

7. All planets
   - ☐ a. are fluid planets.
   - ☐ b. orbit around the sun.
   - ☐ c. can spin faster than the Earth.

8. Scientists think that Jupiter
   - ☐ a. is covered with people.
   - ☐ b. might be able to support life.
   - ☐ c. may soon explode.

9. Jupiter has more
   - ☐ a. moons than the Earth does.
   - ☐ b. rings than Saturn does.
   - ☐ c. gravity than the sun does.

10. Spacecraft help scientists by
   - ☐ a. landing on Jupiter's surface.
   - ☐ b. proving that there is life on Jupiter.
   - ☐ c. taking tests and pictures.

4 Food Smart

A car needs fuel, or gas, in its engine in order to run. Your body also needs fuel, or food, in order to work for you. Eating the *right* kinds of food is wise. You can help your body grow strong by caring about what you eat.

A good place to start is with the four basic food groups. The dairy group has foods like milk, cheese, and yogurt. The other three groups are the meat and fish group, the fruit and vegetable group, and the bread and cereal group. Each meal should have at least one food from all four basic groups. The right combination of these foods will give you needed energy during the day.

It is easy to slip into bad eating habits. You may skip breakfast to get to school or work on time. Or you may not have time for a good lunch. It may seem easy to fill up on potato chips and candy bars from a snack machine. But you may find yourself feeling tired on these days. Often you are unable to think as clearly. It is hard to pay attention to studies. These signs are telling you to take time to eat correctly.

Checking what you eat for one week is a good way to improve your food habits. You may be surprised at what food groups you leave out of meals. Snacking can also be a big problem. When we think of snacks, foods like ice cream, cookies, and cake come to mind. There are many snack foods that are better for your health, however. Carrots, cheese and crackers, fruits, and nuts are just a few of the foods that are healthful snacks. Sweets can still have their place in your diet. But it is better to eat them along with a balanced meal. Foods with lots of sugar should not be eaten in place of the basic foods.

It is important to be aware of what you drink. Too much soda is not good for your body. The calcium from milk is needed for strong bones and teeth. Vitamins in milk and juice will add nutrition to your diet.

Watching what you eat will help keep your body healthy and strong. It is good to get exercise as well. Using your muscles in physical activities will strengthen them. This keeps your heart healthy and builds your stamina. Combining exercise with good eating habits is the key to health.

Recalling Facts

1. Each meal should include food from the
   - ☐ a. two basic food groups.
   - ☐ b. four basic food groups.
   - ☐ c. four basic snack groups.

2. Food directly supplies our bodies with
   - ☐ a. energy.
   - ☐ b. blood.
   - ☐ c. oxygen.

3. Milk is more healthful than soda because it
   - ☐ a. is fresh.
   - ☐ b. provides calcium.
   - ☐ c. tastes better.

4. Milk, cheese, and yogurt are in the
   - ☐ a. vegetable and fruit group.
   - ☐ b. bread and cereal group.
   - ☐ c. dairy group.

5. Checking what you eat for a week is a good way to
   - ☐ a. improve your food habits.
   - ☐ b. watch your weight.
   - ☐ c. plan your mealtimes.

Understanding the Passage

6. You may feel tired and have trouble thinking clearly if you
   - ☐ a. eat three balanced meals a day.
   - ☐ b. skip meals and eat only snacks.
   - ☐ c. exercise frequently.

7. Sugary desserts can be fine to eat if they are
   - ☐ a. low in protein.
   - ☐ b. eaten with meals.
   - ☐ c. eaten with soda.

8. Eating the right foods will help keep your body
   - ☐ a. well toned.
   - ☐ b. strong and healthy.
   - ☐ c. at the same weight.

9. Milk and juices are better to drink than soda because they
   - ☐ a. have important vitamins.
   - ☐ b. taste better.
   - ☐ c. don't need ice.

10. The article compares food in your body to
    - ☐ a. seeds in the ground.
    - ☐ b. gas in a car.
    - ☐ c. sun on our skin.

5 A Pie in the Face

County fairs are a tradition in New England towns. They offer great entertainment. One popular event is the pie-eating contest. There are different reasons for joining in this event. You may want to try out the prize-winning apple pie. Or perhaps you are accepting a dare from a friend. But, before taking the first mouthful, it is a good idea to remember these guidelines.

First, make sure your stomach is nearly empty of food. Eating a whole pie can be hard on the insides if you have just finished a meal. Next, it is helpful to like the pie you are going to eat. Blueberry is a big favorite. But it is messier than other pies. The cream types are another choice. They slide down the throat more easily. Placing your hands in the right position adds to the chances of winning a ribbon. There is a temptation to reach out and help the eating process. This will result in becoming disqualified. Don't just sit on your hands. If your hands are tied behind your back, you will not be tempted to make use of them.

Now you are ready to show your talent at eating pies. The object, of course, is to get to the bottom of the pie plate before the other contestants. It is usually better to start at the outside and work toward the middle. This method gives you a goal to focus on. Try not to notice what the other contestants near you are doing. The important word in this contest is speed. Let the cheers from the crowd spur you on, but do not look up. All you should think about is eating that pie.

When the final bell rings, everyone must stop gobbling. To win you must have finished with your pie. At this point you cannot worry about how you look. Simply smile broadly at the judges, even though your face may be covered with banana cream. Next, you will want a wet towel to wipe away the tasty remains. A tall glass of ice water will taste great. Relax under a shady tree and let your body recover from the strange experience. Eating this fast is not normal.

There is one more important thing to remember. When taking part in this game, be sure to have fun. Now go slice yourself another piece of pie!

Recalling Facts

1. A pie-eating contest is an event at a
   - ☐ a. gas station.
   - ☐ b. county fair.
   - ☐ c. shopping center.

2. Before entering a pie-eating contest you should
   - ☐ a. talk with the judges.
   - ☐ b. have your hair done.
   - ☐ c. not have just eaten.

3. Your hands should be
   - ☐ a. on the table.
   - ☐ b. tied behind your back.
   - ☐ c. in your lap.

4. When eating the pie you should
   - ☐ a. watch what people next to you are doing.
   - ☐ b. work from the outside toward the middle.
   - ☐ c. look at the crowd.

5. The important word in this contest is
   - ☐ a. speed.
   - ☐ b. crowds.
   - ☐ c. blueberries.

Understanding the Passage

6. Cream pies are a good choice because they
   - ☐ a. taste better.
   - ☐ b. are easier to swallow.
   - ☐ c. always win first prize.

7. This story suggests that
   - ☐ a. people always eat a whole pie at once.
   - ☐ b. it is better to eat without your hands.
   - ☐ c. it isn't a good idea to eat so fast all the time.

8. It is important to like the pie you are eating because
   - ☐ a. it will look better on your face.
   - ☐ b. it will be easier to eat.
   - ☐ c. you will have to take it home with you.

9. If you watch the people next to you,
   - ☐ a. they will eat your pie.
   - ☐ b. you might want to have the pie they are eating.
   - ☐ c. you will not have a good chance of winning.

10. County fairs are a way to
    - ☐ a. have a good time.
    - ☐ b. help you lose weight.
    - ☐ c. learn about judging.

When the warm weather arrives, the outdoors blossoms with activity. Birds will sing until dark. Children spend hours playing outside. And the sound of buzzing bees is often heard.

Bees look innocent, but many people are still afraid of them. Bees can give painful, and to some people, fatal stings. But they don't sting unless they are scared or hurt. A bee's stinger is its only means of self-defense. A bee sting may hurt a person, but the bee will die a few hours after using its stinger. The bee's stinger, which is attached to its nervous system, is forced into its victim's body. The bee can't function without a stinger and dies.

When you are stung by a bee, poison enters your body. Immediately scrape off the stinger. Letting it stay in your body will allow more poison to enter. You may feel pain and have some swelling, but you probably won't be uncomfortable for long. A few people, however, are very sensitive to bee stings. Just one sting could cause death. These people must be treated by a doctor right away.

Although there are 10,000 different kinds of bees, the honeybee is the most useful to people. Honeybees make wax and honey. The wax is used to make such products as lipsticks and candles. The honey is good for cooking and for making foods sweet.

When honeybees fly from flower to flower, they help people and the plant. Many fruits and vegetables would die out if bees did not help fertilize flowers. Bees gather nectar and pollen from flowers. They make honey from the nectar and use the honey and pollen as food. Honeybees have a separate honey stomach to carry nectar to the nest.

Honeybees live and work together in large groups. These groups are called colonies, and may have thousands of members. One honeybee may live just a few weeks or months. But a colony may go on living for years. As a group, the honeybees can do many things. They gather water and food. They build homes. They store honey and pollen and eat it when cold weather sets in. Honeybees can even air-condition their hive.

Even though people have studied honeybees' habits for hundreds of years, much is still a mystery. We don't know how the bees know when to work, or how they decide to build more honeycomb. We do know that they are highly organized creatures.

Recalling Facts

1. Bees can give painful
   - ☐ a. stings.
   - ☐ b. rashes.
   - ☐ c. bites.

2. Some people are very sensitive to
   - ☐ a. milk.
   - ☐ b. poison ivy.
   - ☐ c. bee stings.

3. Honeybees make
   - ☐ a. wax and honey.
   - ☐ b. wax and pollen.
   - ☐ c. pollen and honey.

4. The groups honeybees live in are called
   - ☐ a. communities.
   - ☐ b. organizations.
   - ☐ c. colonies.

5. Honeybees know how to
   - ☐ a. find shortcuts to flowers.
   - ☐ b. air-condition their hive.
   - ☐ c. fly in the rain.

Understanding the Passage

6. The poison in a bee's sting
   - ☐ a. can kill some people.
   - ☐ b. doesn't affect children.
   - ☐ c. is easily replaced.

7. Some types of bees
   - ☐ a. have nests in mud.
   - ☐ b. make lipsticks and candles.
   - ☐ c. do not make honey.

8. A single honeybee could not
   - ☐ a. build a beehive.
   - ☐ b. fly from flower to flower.
   - ☐ c. sting a person.

9. A honeybee has more than one
   - ☐ a. stomach.
   - ☐ b. stinger.
   - ☐ c. mother.

10. People don't understand how bees make
    - ☐ a. homes.
    - ☐ b. decisions.
    - ☐ c. honey.

I'll be right back

5 minute

7/10

7   A Gallon Saved

There are more than 100 million cars in the United States. A normal car gets less than 15 miles from each gallon of gas. It travels about 10,000 miles each year. In that time, it uses about 650 gallons of gas. In all, autos use up some 70 billion gallons of gas a year. That comes out to be four-and-a-half million barrels a day.

The importance of saving gas, then, cannot be stressed too much. Let's say, for instance, that the fuel used by each car could be cut back just 15 percent. This could be done by making fewer trips each day. It could be done by keeping autos in good shape. It could be done through better driving habits. If it were done, our nation's use of fuel would fall by close to two-thirds of a million barrels per day.

We can all help to save gas. One way is to ride the buses. Some of us could walk to work. We could ride mopeds or bikes. Another way is to share a ride. We could join carpools. About one-third of all cars are used for going to and from work.

Go shopping with a friend from time to time. If two people use a car instead of one, we all save. Driving stress would be less, too, with fewer cars on the road. The savings on gas around the nation would come to more than one-half million barrels a day.

Another way to save is by cutting out useless trips. Can you find one car trip per week that could be handled by telephone? Can you combine trips? If each car took one less 10-mile trip a week, we could save three-and-a-half billion gallons of gas a year. This comes to nearly 5 percent of the total passenger car demand for gas.

The way people drive decides how much fuel they save. Careful drivers may get 20 percent more miles per gallon than normal drivers. They could get 50 percent more miles per gallon than wasteful drivers. Careful drivers obey the 55-mile-per-hour speed limit. They get to their desired speed quickly and keep a steady pace.

If just one gallon of gas were saved each week for each car in the country, we could all save about five-and-a-half billion gallons a year.

Recalling Facts

1. There are more than 100
   million cars in
   □ a. Canada.
   □ b. Europe.
   □ c. the United States.

2. An average car travels 10,000
   miles each
   □ a. week.
   □ b. month.
   □ c. year.

3. Keeping your car in good
   shape helps you save
   □ a. coal.
   □ b. gas.
   □ c. water.

4. About one-third of all private
   cars are used for going to
   and from
   □ a. school.
   □ b. vacations.
   □ c. work.

5. To do away with useless car
   trips, you can use the
   □ a. dictionary.
   □ b. library.
   □ c. telephone.

Understanding the Passage

6. What is the main idea of
   this article?
   □ a. Americans need to save gas.
   □ b. Gas prices continue to rise.
   □ c. Small cars get good gas
   mileage.

7. A typical car gets 15 miles to the
   gallon. This figure is
   □ a. an average.
   □ b. a guess.
   □ c. a minimum.

8. Sharing a ride with a friend
   is called
   □ a. carloading.
   □ b. carpooling.
   □ c. cartraveling.

9. If more people shared a ride,
   there would be
   □ a. fewer cars on the road.
   □ b. higher insurance rates.
   □ c. more highway accidents.

10. This article hints that a careful
    driver travels about
    □ a. 55 miles per hour.
    □ b. 65 miles per hour.
    □ c. 75 miles per hour.

8 Decisions, Decisions

Shopping for a carpet or rug? Before you decide, think about how you want your rug to serve you. Do you want it mostly for adding beauty to your home? Do you expect it to hold up under hard wear? Should it be easy to clean? Look for a carpet that suits your taste, needs, and budget.

How much traffic will your carpet get? Carpet in a living room, kitchen, rumpus room, or entrance gets more wear than one in a bedroom or guest room. For these heavy traffic areas, you will want a carpet that wears well. Carpets of lesser quality may be all right for little-used rooms.

Will the carpet be used where children spend a lot of time? Will pets play on it? If so, you know that there will be spills and stains. Get a carpet that does not stain and is easy to clean.

Will the carpet be near sunlight or dampness? If so, you'll want to be sure its colors won't fade and that its fibers won't mildew.

Think about floor coverage. Wall-to-wall carpet has a grand look and tends to give a room a finished appearance. It hides poor flooring and helps to muffle noise. It won't shift when walked upon. And it has no edges to trip over.

On the other hand, a room-fit carpet is cut nearly to the size of the room. The edges of the floor are left showing. It looks almost like wall-to-wall carpet, but it can be removed for cleaning. And, depending on the shape, it can be turned in order to wear evenly. Room-fit carpet usually needs to be laid by rug experts.

Room-size rugs are sold in standard sizes. These may be 9-by-12 feet or 12-by-15 feet. They are easy to put down. They can be shifted for equal wear. They can be easily removed for cleaning.

Area rugs can be used to fill in a spot or to separate one area from another. They can be used over wall-to-wall carpet in heavy traffic places. They are easy to move.

Scatter rugs are usually smaller than 4-by-6 feet. They come in many shapes and styles. Many are washable. Scatter rugs should have nonskid backing to prevent sliding. Choose your rugs carefully, and you'll be happy with your choice.

Recalling Facts

1. When buying a carpet, you should choose one that suits your taste, needs, and
   - ☐ a. budget.
   - ☐ b. car.
   - ☐ c. personality.

2. A living room carpet gets more wear than one in a
   - ☐ a. bedroom.
   - ☐ b. entrance.
   - ☐ c. kitchen.

3. Which kind of rug won't shift when walked upon?
   - ☐ a. area rug
   - ☐ b. scatter rug
   - ☐ c. wall-to-wall carpet

4. Which of the following is a standard size for a room-size rug?
   - ☐ a. 4-by-5
   - ☐ b. 9-by-12
   - ☐ c. 8-by-13

5. Many styles of scatter rugs are
   - ☐ a. expensive.
   - ☐ b. returnable.
   - ☐ c. washable.

Understanding the Passage

6. A carpet of lesser quality might be used in the
   - ☐ a. kitchen.
   - ☐ b. rumpus room.
   - ☐ c. guest room.

7. For a room where children spend a lot of time, you should get a carpet that is
   - ☐ a. easy to clean.
   - ☐ b. germ free.
   - ☐ c. soft and warm.

8. Sunlight might make a carpet
   - ☐ a. fade.
   - ☐ b. shrink.
   - ☐ c. mildew.

9. To keep the noise level in a room down, you should choose
   - ☐ a. area rugs.
   - ☐ b. scatter rugs.
   - ☐ c. wall-to-wall carpet.

10. Scatter rugs should have nonskid backing to prevent a person from
    - ☐ a. breaking into the house.
    - ☐ b. setting the rug on fire.
    - ☐ c. slipping and falling down.

9   A Greek Hero

Ulysses was a great hero in Greek mythology. Both the Greeks and the Romans wrote many tales about him. Sometimes the stories portrayed him as a noble. But many writers thought of him as a lying trickster. The most famous stories about Ulysses were written by the Greek poet Homer.

Homer's Ulysses was the king of Ithaca, one of the most famous cities in Greece. He married a woman named Penelope. But Greek leaders would not let Ulysses rule his kingdom in peace. They wanted him to join their war against the city of Troy.

Ulysses did not want to fight. Trying to fool the Greeks, he pretended that he was insane. Instead of planting seeds in his field, he planted salt. But the Greeks knew that Ulysses was faking. They took his baby son and put him in the path of the plow. Ulysses turned the plow to the side in order to save his son's life. In this way, the Greeks proved that Ulysses was really sane.

Ulysses agreed to sail with the Greek army to Troy. During the Trojan War, he was a brave fighter. He was also a wise counselor to the Greek leaders. He was greatly honored by the Greeks at the end of the war.

After ten years of fighting, the Greeks finally won the Trojan War. Ulysses set sail for home. But it took him another ten years to get there. He encountered many adventures on the way. At one point, he was captured in the land of the Cyclops. The Cyclops was a one-eyed giant. After he set sail again, he was caught by a beautiful witch named Circe. Finally, the help of the goddess Athena brought him home to his wife and son.

It had been twenty years since Ulysses had left Ithaca. Several noblemen tried to convince Penelope that her husband was really dead. They moved into Ulysses's palace. The men demanded that Penelope marry one of them. But she did not believe her husband was dead. By thinking up tricks to fool the noblemen, Penelope remained faithful to Ulysses. But after twenty years, she began to run out of tricks.

The queen said that she would hold an archery contest. Whoever won the contest could marry her. Ulysses arrived home the day before the contest. He entered the archery bout and won. Then Ulysses was finally reunited with his family.

Recalling Facts

1. The most famous stories about Ulysses were written by
   □ a. Penelope.
   □ b. the Romans.
   □ c. Homer.

2. Ulysses was the king of
   □ a. Greece.
   □ b. Ithaca.
   □ c. Troy.

3. Ulysses pretended that he was
   □ a. unhappy.
   □ b. hungry.
   □ c. insane.

4. The Trojan War lasted for
   □ a. ten years.
   □ b. twenty years.
   □ c. thirty years.

5. Circe was
   □ a. Ulysses's wife.
   □ b. a witch.
   □ c. a Cyclops.

Understanding the Passage

6. Homer wrote
   □ a. the only stories about Ulysses.
   □ b. all the Greek myths.
   □ c. one version of Ulysses's life.

7. The Greeks and Trojans
   □ a. were enemies.
   □ b. fought on the same side.
   □ c. believed Ulysses was insane.

8. Ulysses was grateful for the help of
   □ a. the Trojans.
   □ b. the noblemen.
   □ c. Athena.

9. Penelope wanted to
   □ a. marry a nobleman.
   □ b. be a widow.
   □ c. wait for her husband.

10. Ulysses was the
    □ a. oldest man in the archery contest.
    □ b. best archer in the contest.
    □ c. only archer competing.

A Small Country

Andorra, one of the smallest countries in the world, is located high in the mountains between France and Spain. The country covers only 179 square miles. That is less than half the size of New York City. About 43,000 people live in Andorra.

High, rocky mountains surround Andorra. Until the 1930s, travelers had difficulty reaching the country. Up until that time, people in Andorra lived the way they had lived for centuries. Most Andorrans worked as farmers or as shepherds. Things did not change quickly.

When roads were built from France and Spain to Andorra in the 1930s, life picked up speed. Tourists began to visit the small country. These tourists brought in a lot of money to spend while visiting. Many people in Andorra found new jobs in shops or hotels. These changes helped to keep young people in Andorra. There were many more jobs than before the roads were built.

Today tourists provide 80 to 90 percent of Andorra's income. More than a million people visit each year. They come to view the rugged mountains. They enjoy the quiet way of life. Most people are also interested in the ancient buildings. There are many shops for tourists to browse in. Clothes, watches, jewelry, wines, and other items are sold at low prices in Andorra. Import fees are low, so tourists enjoy the inexpensive shopping.

Most of the businesses in Andorra are owned by its citizens. There are not many foreign businesses. Some Andorrans still farm and graze sheep and cattle. But most are now involved with the tourist trade.

Andorra has an unusual legal system. It is based on ancient laws and rules. The country is ruled by a Spanish bishop and the president of France. They are called the "princes of Andorra." They have equal power and must agree before any change can be made in Andorra. The two rulers have been paid for their services in the same way for centuries. Every two years, the bishop of Spain receives 6 hams, 6 cheeses, 12 hens, and 8 dollars. The president of France is paid 2 dollars every other year.

As well as having two rulers, Andorra has two sets of public services. There are two postal services. One is French and one is Spanish. There are two school systems as well. People in Andorra speak French and Spanish. But their official language is called *Catalan*.

Recalling Facts

1. Andorra is located between France and
   - ☐ a. England.
   - ☐ b. Spain.
   - ☐ c. Sicily.

2. Before the 1930s, Andorra was
   - ☐ a. cut off from the rest of the world.
   - ☐ b. a major center for tourism.
   - ☐ c. very easy to get to.

3. Andorra covers only
   - ☐ a. 59 square miles.
   - ☐ b. 179 square miles.
   - ☐ c. 279 square miles.

4. Tourists provide 80 to 90 percent of Andorra's
   - ☐ a. employers.
   - ☐ b. shops.
   - ☐ c. income.

5. Andorra has two sets of
   - ☐ a. school systems.
   - ☐ b. bus systems.
   - ☐ c. employment systems.

Understanding the Passage

6. Andorra is
   - ☐ a. larger than New York City.
   - ☐ b. smaller than New York City.
   - ☐ c. the same size as New York City.

7. Most people in Andorra work
   - ☐ a. as farmers.
   - ☐ b. in shops.
   - ☐ c. in factories.

8. Andorra's economy changed when
   - ☐ a. roads were built.
   - ☐ b. shopkeepers moved away.
   - ☐ c. schools were improved.

9. The legal system in Andorra is
   - ☐ a. fairly modern.
   - ☐ b. very old.
   - ☐ c. seldom used.

10. A main attraction for visitors to Andorra is the
    - ☐ a. mountains.
    - ☐ b. fish markets.
    - ☐ c. restaurants.

Have Tent Will Travel

Shall we take a tent? That is the overnight camper's question. A bed beneath the stars sounds nice. But sometimes it's not practical. Most campers carry some kind of shelter. No one likes to wake up with rain or snow in the face or a soggy sleeping bag. Besides, there are many kinds of lightweight tents made for campers. Some have a floor and a netting over the entrance. This makes them insect-proof, animal-proof, and waterproof. Stakes need not be much larger than a nail. Aluminum poles fold and can be packed within the tent. All in all, a shelter can be quite compact.

However, the fabric for the tent can be a problem. A nylon tent is light to carry, but it can hold moisture inside the tent and cause dampness. Waterproof cotton, on the other hand, isn't completely watertight. Campers solve the problem by using a cloth tent and placing a nylon or plastic cover over it. A shelter need not be a tent. A nylon groundcloth or a large piece of plastic can be tied up to trees to give shelter. A poncho can be used for the same purpose.

When camping, pick a good campsite. An unnoticed gully could turn into a waterway if it rains during the night. A gentle stream can become a chilly neighbor at night. Choose a place where there is drinking water. Look for sources of fuelwood and try for level ground. If you're lucky, you might even find a place with a view. Pitch your tent where it can get the morning sun. This way, it will dry out before you have to pack it away. Note where the wind is coming from before pitching your tent. The wind will blow off a lake and onto the shore at night. During the day, the wind will blow the other way. In some places, rain is rare and tents are not needed. A nice spot would be a rocky ledge that holds in the heat and blocks the night winds. An overhanging branch will provide a natural roof and clothes hooks. Don't camp under dead branches or in the path of rock slides.

When breaking camp, be sure that your fire is out. Dump water on the ashes. Stir them in with the soil until you are sure that all of the embers are wet.

Recalling Facts

1. Most overnight campers carry some kind of
   - ☐ a. map.
   - ☐ b. shelter.
   - ☐ c. weapon.

2. Some tents have a netting over the
   - ☐ a. entrance.
   - ☐ b. roof.
   - ☐ c. wall.

3. The problem with a nylon tent is that it may
   - ☐ a. burn easily.
   - ☐ b. hold moisture.
   - ☐ c. be heavy.

4. Waterproof cotton tents are not
   - ☐ a. insect-proof.
   - ☐ b. lightweight.
   - ☐ c. watertight.

5. Before you leave your campsite, it is important to
   - ☐ a. eat a good breakfast.
   - ☐ b. wash off your tent.
   - ☐ c. put out your fire.

Understanding the Passage

6. When you go camping, it's a good idea to take along some type of
   - ☐ a. guide.
   - ☐ b. pet.
   - ☐ c. shelter.

7. Aluminum poles are
   - ☐ a. heavy.
   - ☐ b. lightweight.
   - ☐ c. waterproof.

8. Nylon tents
   - ☐ a. are very heavy.
   - ☐ b. do not weigh much.
   - ☐ c. keep animals away.

9. When you choose a campsite, it's a good idea not to camp near a
   - ☐ a. rock.
   - ☐ b. stream.
   - ☐ c. town.

10. This article hints that you should
   - ☐ a. choose your campsite carefully.
   - ☐ b. never go camping alone.
   - ☐ c. stay in your car when you can.

12 Solar Power

Solar energy for your home is coming. It can help you as a single home owner. It can help the whole country as well. Whether or not solar energy can save you money depends on many things. Where you live is one factor. The type of home you have is another. Things like insulation, present energy costs, and the type of system you buy are added factors.

Using solar energy can help save our precious fuel. As you know, our supplies of oil and gas are very limited. There is just not enough on hand to meet all our future energy needs. And when Mother Nature says that's all, that's all. The only way we can delay hearing those words is by starting to save energy now and by using other sources, like the sun.

We won't have to worry about the sun's running out of energy for another several billion years or so. Besides being an endless source of energy, the use of the sun has other advantages as well. The sun does not offer as many problems as other energy sources. For example, fossil fuel plants add to already high pollution levels. With solar energy, we will still need these sources of energy, but we won't need as much. That means we can cut down on our pollution problems.

With all these good points, why don't we use more solar power? There are many reasons for this. The biggest reason is money. Until now, it was just not practical for a homeowner to put in a solar unit. There were cheaper sources of energy. All that is changing now. Solar costs are starting to equal the costs of oil and electricity. Experts say that gas, oil, and electricity prices will continue to rise. The demand for electricity is increasing rapidly. But new power plants will use more gas, oil, or coal. Already in some places the supply of electricity is being rationed.

Solar energy is now in its infancy. It could soon grow to become a major part of our nation's energy supply.

Recalling Facts

1. Whether or not solar
   energy will save you
   money depends on
   ☐ a. family size.
   ☐ b. where you live.
   ☐ c. your income.

2. Solar energy can help us save
   precious
   ☐ a. fuel.
   ☐ b. plants.
   ☐ c. soil.

3. The sun will not run out of
   energy for several
   ☐ a. thousand years.
   ☐ b. million years.
   ☐ c. billion years.

4. Solar energy will help cut
   down on
   ☐ a. food.
   ☐ b. pollution.
   ☐ c. traffic.

5. The biggest reason for
   not using more solar power
   now is
   ☐ a. money.
   ☐ b. time.
   ☐ c. space.

Understanding the Passage

6. What is this article about?
   ☐ a. energy from the sun
   ☐ b. natural gas
   ☐ c. how oil is made

7. What does this article suggest?
   ☐ a. Oil companies are against
      solar energy.
   ☐ b. Many people are afraid of
      solar energy.
   ☐ c. Solar energy might ease the
      energy problem.

8. Solar energy causes
   ☐ a. less pollution than oil.
   ☐ b. more pollution than oil.
   ☐ c. the same pollution as oil.

9. People who install solar units will
   not have to worry about
   ☐ a. insulating their homes.
   ☐ b. long gas lines.
   ☐ c. running short of fuel.

10. In the future, the price of gas
    and oil will
    ☐ a. come down.
    ☐ b. go up.
    ☐ c. stay the same.

13   Alcoholism

Alcoholism is a serious disease. It affects many people. Nearly nine million Americans alone suffer from the illness. Alcoholism takes many different forms. Sometimes the disease means constant drinking. Other times it involves periods of heavy drinking. Many scientists disagree about what the differences are between an alcoholic and a social drinker. The difference occurs when someone needs to drink, and this need gets in the way of his health or behavior.

Alcohol causes a loss of judgment and alertness. After a long period, alcoholism can deteriorate the liver, the brain, and other parts of the body. Alcoholism can also result in death. The illness is dangerous because it is involved in half of all automobile accidents. Another problem is that the victim often denies being an alcoholic and won't get help.

Solutions do exist. Many hospitals and centers treat withdrawal and help patients cope. Support groups listen. Counselors offer advice. Without assistance the victim can destroy his life. Alcoholism also affects family and friends. A sufferer often tries to hide the problems. He will detach himself from the routines of life. He may lose his employment, home, or loved ones.

All the causes of the sickness are not discovered yet. There is no standard for a person with alcoholism. Victims range in age, race, sex, and background. There is some evidence that relatives of alcoholics are at risk. They may not in fact be victims. However they should realize possible dangers. Many people with this problem don't like themselves or their lives. Men and women both can become alcoholics. Men do more often. Some groups of people are more vulnerable to the illness. People from broken homes and North American Indians are two examples. People from broken homes often lack stable lives. Indians may also lack this because they have been transported so often. In history, the white settlers tried to calm the angry Indians with alcohol so they would not fight. The problem has now been passed on.

Alcoholism is clearly present in society today. People have started to get help and information. With proper assistance, victims can put their lives together one day at a time. The public must continue to help those affected by this disease. If everyone admits there is a problem and offers support, then alcoholism can be decreased. The process will be slow, but it can be done.

Recalling Facts

1. The number of American alcoholics is
   - ☐ a. less than two million.
   - ☐ b. nearly nine million.
   - ☐ c. sixty thousand.

2. One of the problems with alcoholism is
   - ☐ a. denial by the victim.
   - ☐ b. it forces others to drink.
   - ☐ c. friends can catch the disease through contact.

3. Alcoholism can result in
   - ☐ a. a good time.
   - ☐ b. overeating and overweight.
   - ☐ c. harm to the liver, brain, and other parts of the body.

4. Alcoholics differ in
   - ☐ a. age.
   - ☐ b. race.
   - ☐ c. both of the above.

5. Which of the following are most at risk?
   - ☐ a. Europeans
   - ☐ b. people from broken homes
   - ☐ c. children under the age of five

Understanding the Passage

6. The main difference between an alcoholic and a social drinker is that
   - ☐ a. an alcoholic is dependent on alcohol.
   - ☐ b. an alcoholic drinks in the daytime.
   - ☐ c. a social drinker never gets drunk.

7. An alcoholic can find help
   - ☐ a. with more alcohol.
   - ☐ b. by himself.
   - ☐ c. through support groups and counselors.

8. Relatives of alcoholics should
   - ☐ a. never pick up a drink themselves.
   - ☐ b. be aware of the dangers and warning signs of this disease.
   - ☐ c. blame other family members.

9. Settlers introduced Indians to alcohol in order to
   - ☐ a. weaken their fighting powers.
   - ☐ b. celebrate the harvest.
   - ☐ c. welcome the Indians to their new home.

10. The author believes that
    - ☐ a. alcoholics will always be hopeless failures.
    - ☐ b. America must ignore the problem of alcoholism.
    - ☐ c. with support and help, alcoholics can deal with their disease and lead normal lives.

14 The Art of Pressing Flowers

A flower garden with its bright plants is a lovely sight. A bouquet of pretty flowers will make a friend smile. We know flowers cannot last. But there is a way to keep some of their beauty. This is called fleurage. It is the art of pressing flowers to keep some of their beauty.

You can either press whole flowers or single petals. This depends on what type of flowers you use. First, divide the flowers. Place each flower between paper-lined pages of large books. The paper between the pages will blot the flowers dry. The texture of the paper used will change the look of the ● petals. For instance, if you use a rough paper towel, the pattern will transfer to the flower. A soft facial tissue will create a more natural look.

The books should be kept in a warm, dry place. Wait two weeks. The petals should now be dry enough for use. They will feel much like paper. You are now ready to make a design. It is best to start by making an outline with pencil. The next step is to glue the petals in the outlined space. A nonacid white glue is the best choice for this project. You want to make ● sure the picture will last.

The rest of this process is up to you. It is what makes each design different. You can use whole petals or you can tear them into various shapes. Some flowers, such as the iris, are very fragile. Roses and daffodils are also among those that need careful handling. You will want to decide on a choice of colors. You can create a picture resembling an actual flower garden. Or, the design can be a collage of beautiful shades joined together. When the work is done, pick out a frame to give it just the right look. These ● pictures are great for gift giving. But, you may want to keep them for yourself.

It is normal for the petals in your picture to fade. This will add a special effect to the design. It is a good idea, however, to hang your work away from the sun.

The next time you receive a bouquet of flowers, don't throw them away. Practice the art of fleurage. It is a wonderful way to keep the beauty of flowers. This type of bouquet lasts forever. And it never needs water!

Recalling Facts

1. The art of pressing flowers is called
   □ a. origami.
   □ b. fleurage.
   □ c. gluing petals.

2. The texture of the paper used for drying will
   □ a. tear the petals.
   □ b. change the look of the petals.
   □ c. make the petals wetter.

3. Petals can be taken out of the books after about
   □ a. one day.
   □ b. one month.
   □ c. two weeks.

4. Before making your design, it is best to
   □ a. outline with pencil.
   □ b. put glue on the petals.
   □ c. throw the flowers away.

5. After the picture is finished, it is normal for the petals to
   □ a. peel off.
   □ b. turn to glue.
   □ c. fade.

Understanding the Passage

6. Fleurage is a way to
   □ a. have fun with glue.
   □ b. keep a flower's beauty.
   □ c. practice making pictures.

7. Using a nonacid white glue will
   □ a. help the picture last longer.
   □ b. tear the petals.
   □ c. make the petals fade.

8. It is best to work carefully because
   □ a. you will run out of glue.
   □ b. some petals are very fragile.
   □ c. petals tear after two minutes.

9. Using paper between the book pages
   □ a. will help dry the petals.
   □ b. is a way to design the picture.
   □ c. makes the petals stick better.

10. Outlining the design first
    □ a. means the petals are not dry enough.
    □ b. helps in placement of the petals.
    □ c. causes the petals to fade.

15 Beach Sense

Take a walk on the beach. The beach is one of the best places to become aware of all of your senses. Just by walking you are using the sense of touch. Notice the changing texture of the sand as you leave footprints behind. Close to the shore, the water reaches out and laps your toes with its coolness. The sun kisses your skin with glowing warmth. The light sea breeze plays with your hair.

Breathe in the smell of the ocean. The smell of salty air mixed with seaweed is a unique blend. If you are lucky enough to be near a fishing boat you may pick up scent of the day's seafood catch. Smoke drifts toward you as families prepare a meal on a charcoal grill.

There are numerous sounds heard at the beach. Waves crash like cymbals as they rush toward the shore. Seagulls squawk loudly, flying in low circles over the water. Voices and laughter rise and fall with the tides. Sometimes you can hear a boat motor growl in the distance.

Your eyes are kept busy taking in many sights at the beach. There are a number of shells to look at and examine. It is fun to watch people involved in their own activities. Some are swimming. Others are building sandcastles. A group may be playing volleyball or Frisbee, or flying kites. And then there are the bronzed bodies stretched out beneath the sun. At the end of the day it is soothing to watch the waves roll in and out. When night falls, the moon reflected on the sea is a special sight.

You may think the sense of taste isn't accounted for at the beach. But have you ever been caught by the force of a wild wave? When that happens, it is hard to avoid a swallow of salt water. This is definitely not a pleasant taste. But a day at the beach isn't complete unless you have at least one gulp. Younger children will be happy to tell you about the flavor of sand. And any food seems to taste better when eaten at the seashore.

Of all five senses, your sense of hearing is the one most used while at the beach. Sit quietly at the shore. Listen to the ocean make its special music as the waves crest and break. The sound of the ever-flowing tides is reason enough to visit the beach again.

Recalling Facts

1. The beach is a good place to become aware of your
   - ☐ a. friends.
   - ☑ b. senses.
   - ☐ c. feet.

2. A common type of boat seen near the ocean is a
   - ☑ a. fishing boat.
   - ☐ b. riverboat.
   - ☐ c. canoe.

3. A bird that can be seen at the beach is a
   - ☐ a. cardinal.
   - ☑ b. seagull.
   - ☐ c. hummingbird.

4. The beach is a good place to look for
   - ☑ a. shells.
   - ☐ b. gold.
   - ☐ c. charcoal.

5. The sense that is most used at the beach is
   - ☐ a. taste.
   - ☑ b. touch.
   - ☐ c. hearing.

Understanding the Passage

6. Footprints make impressions along the beach because the
   - ☑ a. sand is wet.
   - ☐ b. ocean is cold.
   - ☐ c. tides are different.

7. A smell unique to the seaside is
   - ☐ a. hot dogs cooking.
   - ☑ b. seaweed and salt air.
   - ☐ c. charcoal burning in a grill.

8. People do not generally use time at the beach for
   - ☑ a. sunbathing.
   - ☐ b. working.
   - ☐ c. playing volleyball.

9. Very few people spend a day at the beach without
   - ☐ a. eating a hamburger.
   - ☑ b. getting sunburned.
   - ☐ c. tasting salt water.

10. Ocean tides
    - ☐ a. occur only once in a while.
    - ☑ b. are constantly flowing.
    - ☐ c. create difficulties in traffic.

16 Surviving Is No Accident

Good transportation is very important in the winter. If you have a car, make sure it is ready for the cold weather. Your car should be in top working order all year round. But, when winter comes, take extra care.

Keep the gas tank as nearly full as you can. This will keep water out of the tank and will be a reserve in case you get into trouble. A winter car kit is also a good idea. It should contain blankets, matches, and candles. It should have tools, a first-aid kit, tire chains, sand, and a shovel. Other useful items would be a flashlight with extra batteries and a small food supply of canned nuts and candy.

If you must drive in a storm, you should plan your trip in advance. Pick a first and a second route. Listen to the radio before starting out. Get the latest news on the storm. Try not to drive alone. If you can, take two or three others with you. Try also to travel along with another car. If the storm becomes too much for you to drive in, seek shelter right away.

If a storm traps you in your car, there are some steps you should take for your own safety. Do not attempt to walk to find help. You may quickly lose your way in blowing and drifting snow. Being lost in open country is very dangerous. Your chances of being found are better if you stay in your car. It can be your shelter while you wait.

Keep a downwind window open slightly for fresh air. Freezing rain can seal off your car and lock you inside. Run the engine and heater once in a while. Keep the same downwind window open while the engine is running. Make sure that snow has not blocked the exhaust pipe. Clap your hands and move your arms and legs from time to time. Do not stay in one position too long. But do not move too much. Exercise warms you up, but it also causes you to lose body heat.

If more than one person is in the car, do not sleep at the same time. One person should always be awake. If you are alone, stay awake as long as you can. Turn on the inside light at night. This will make your car more visible to working crews. Don't panic. Stay with your car.

Recalling Facts

1. In winter, you should keep
   your gas tank
   □ a. a quarter full.
   □ b. half full.
   □ c. almost full.

2. A winter car kit should
   contain
   □ a. blankets.
   □ b. books.
   □ c. paper.

3. If you must drive in a storm,
   you should
   □ a. drive alone.
   □ b. plan your trip.
   □ c. turn off the radio.

4. If you are trapped in your car,
   you should make sure that the
   snow does not block the
   □ a. bumpers.
   □ b. exhaust pipe.
   □ c. wheels.

5. Exercise causes you
   to lose body
   □ a. fluids.
   □ b. heat.
   □ c. tone.

Understanding the Passage

6. Freezing rain can cause
   □ a. the gas tank to explode.
   □ b. the car to leak.
   □ c. you to be trapped in
      your car.

7. Your car should be in top working
   order, especially during the
   □ a. summer.
   □ b. fall.
   □ c. winter.

8. If a storm traps you in your car,
   you should not
   □ a. leave your car.
   □ b. open a window.
   □ c. run your engine.

9. The best advice when traveling in
   winter is to
   □ a. be prepared.
   □ b. travel alone.
   □ c. wear warm clothes.

10. This article hints that in a storm
    □ a. car radios are unimportant.
    □ b. road maps are of little use.
    □ c. too much exercise is harmful.

17 Mary, Queen of Scots

The tragic tale of Mary, Queen of Scots began at her birth in 1542. When the princess was a week old, her father died. The infant was proclaimed queen of Scotland. Mary's mother saw that her child could never lead a normal life. So when Mary was five, she was sent to France. There she would be taught how to rule Scotland.

Mary was only fifteen when she married. Her husband was the crown prince of France. This wedding could unite Scotland and France in friendship. Soon the young prince became king of France. Then suddenly he died.

Mary returned home to Scotland. At the age of nineteen, she was prepared to take charge of her country. But things had changed in Scotland. Once it had been a Catholic country. Now more and more Scots were becoming Protestants. The Catholic queen found that Scotland no longer wanted her.

A few years later, the queen married once more. Her husband, Lord Darnley, was also Catholic. Mary's enemies rebelled against his rise to power. This was the queen's first brush with trouble. Her enemies were quelled, but many problems still remained. On top of these, she and her husband were unhappy together.

Mary gave birth to a son named James. But she still disliked her husband. He was a weak ruler, and he was cruel to her friends. One day, there was a great explosion at Darnley's house. He was found dead. Many Scots thought the crime had been planned. They blamed the Earl of Bothwell. And the Earl was a close friend of the queen.

After Lord Darnley was killed, the queen married the Earl of Bothwell. Mary was forced to leave the throne. Her son James became king of Scotland. In exile, she became the center of a secret plot. Mary and her new husband planned to kill the queen of England. They wanted all of Britain to be one Catholic country. The queen of England learned of this plot. She was a Protestant and hated Mary. The two queens kept up a bitter feud. Finally Queen Elizabeth of England captured Mary. She kept the Scottish queen in prison for a year. But Mary refused to stop plotting against Queen Elizabeth. Even in prison, Mary stayed in touch with her friends.

In 1587, a court found Mary guilty of treason. She was beheaded soon after that.

Recalling Facts

1. When Mary was five, she was sent to
   - ☐ a. Scotland.
   - ☐ b. England.
   - ☐ c. France.

2. The queen of Scotland first married when she was
   - ☐ a. fifteen.
   - ☐ b. five.
   - ☐ c. nineteen.

3. Mary's son was named
   - ☐ a. James.
   - ☐ b. Lord Darnley.
   - ☐ c. Henry.

4. Mary planned to
   - ☐ a. become a Protestant.
   - ☐ b. kill the queen of England.
   - ☐ c. divorce the Earl of Bothwell.

5. The queen of England ordered that Mary be
   - ☐ a. released.
   - ☐ b. pardoned.
   - ☐ c. beheaded.

Understanding the Passage

6. Mary became queen of Scotland
   - ☐ a. after she married.
   - ☐ b. very early in her life.
   - ☐ c. when she was imprisoned.

7. Mary, Queen of Scots married
   - ☐ a. once.
   - ☐ b. twice.
   - ☐ c. three times.

8. Mary obviously
   - ☐ a. hated Protestants.
   - ☐ b. liked Protestants.
   - ☐ c. became a Protestant.

9. Scotland disliked the Earl of Bothwell because he
   - ☐ a. beheaded the queen of Scotland.
   - ☐ b. was a close friend of Mary.
   - ☐ c. fought with France.

10. Queen Elizabeth wanted to
    - ☐ a. marry the Earl of Bothwell.
    - ☐ b. join forces with Mary.
    - ☐ c. keep England a Protestant country.

18 All Aboard for the Vermont Hills

One of the best states in which to view brilliant fall colors is Vermont. The changing leaves add to the beautiful scenery. You can choose from three different railroads to tour the area. Two of the trains are in the northern part of Vermont. One travels along Route 100 near Stowe. The other leaves Route 91 from the town of St. Johnsbury.

Riding a train keeps you away from busy traffic. You are surrounded by spectacular views. You will see fields and rivers that have remained the same for over 70 years.

As you board the train near Stowe, you will feel that you have gone back in time. The conductor greets you in a uniform from the year 1917. Look out the window as the train chugs along the track. You pass small farms with cattle grazing in the fields. The train crosses through the Fisher Bridge near the village of Wolcott. This bridge is very historic. It is one of the last covered railroad bridges in the United States. As you look in wonder, you see sheer rock cliffs plunge to the river below. The train now makes a wide horseshoe curve. It begins a steep eight-mile climb up Walden Mountain. Through the breaks in the trees incredible sights can be seen. At the top, you are 1,700 feet above sea level. This is the second highest railroad summit in New England.

At this point in the trip you may get out and stretch your legs. The engine will be moved to the other end of the train for the return trip. The complete train ride covers 60 miles.

Another great railroad trip starts at the southern end of Vermont. This is the "Rutland Train" operated by the Green Mountain Railroad. This train leaves from Bellows Falls and travels 26 miles through the scenic country-side. This train ride takes you along the Connecticut River. Two covered bridges are also on the train's route. They were built after a terrible flood in 1869. Another grand sight is the expansive gorge and waterfall near Brock-way Mills. You may want to take a picture as the train slows through here.

This tour is also narrated to provide you with some interesting history. These trips are offered in the fall to highlight this lovely season. It is a great way to explore the beautiful state of Vermont.

Recalling Facts

1. Two of the train rides leave from
   - ☐ a. southern New Hampshire.
   - ☐ b. southern Vermont.
   - ☐ c. northern Vermont.

2. The Fisher Bridge is
   - ☐ a. one of the last covered railroad bridges.
   - ☐ b. built over a mountain gorge.
   - ☐ c. over five miles long.

3. For the return trip, the engine is
   - ☐ a. refueled.
   - ☐ b. left in the same position.
   - ☐ c. moved to the other end.

4. The "Rutland Train" starts from
   - ☐ a. Bellows Falls.
   - ☐ b. Rutland.
   - ☐ c. St. Johnsbury.

5. The conductor will
   - ☐ a. narrate the trip.
   - ☐ b. wear a uniform from 1917.
   - ☐ c. park your car.

Understanding the Passage

6. Taking a scenic train ride is a good way to
   - ☐ a. meet people.
   - ☐ b. avoid traffic.
   - ☐ c. get to a high place.

7. The story suggests that Vermont has many
   - ☐ a. historic places.
   - ☐ b. conductors in uniforms.
   - ☐ c. straight roads.

8. Much of the Vermont countryside seems to be
   - ☐ a. quite urban.
   - ☐ b. very hilly.
   - ☐ c. swampland.

9. The train rides are offered in the fall as a way to
   - ☐ a. enjoy the colorful leaves.
   - ☐ b. see the covered bridges.
   - ☐ c. meet the conductor.

10. The beautiful sights in Vermont are a good reason to
   - ☐ a. build covered bridges.
   - ☐ b. take pictures.
   - ☐ c. become a conductor.

19

Fall Safe

Bad falls are the most common form of injury to young infants. A baby is helpless. She needs total care. A child wiggles and rolls. You never know when she will roll over. Her crib, with the sides pulled up, and her playpen are the only safe places for the child to be left alone. A tot should never be left alone on a couch or a bed or any other high place from which she might fall.

If you have to answer the door or the phone, take care of the child first. If you are in the middle of a diaper change, take the baby with you or put her back in the crib. Make it a habit to hold on to the baby if you must reach for something. Always be sure to keep at least one hand on her. Turning your back for even a second can be risky.

When the baby learns to crawl and creep, you must block the tops and bottoms of stairways. One of the most common accidents for babies at this stage is falling down stairs. This happens because babies learn to go up before they learn to go down safely. Safety gates for stairs are sold in many stores. Or you may block the stairs off with something. Anything that the child cannot move will do the job.

When the child begins to walk and climb, you will have to be extra watchful. It is not enough to just tend to her needs. You must also teach her about dangers. A tot wants to look at everything. Open doors and open windows are paths to great danger.

Another problem is falling while you're carrying the baby. Keep stairs free of objects which can cause you to fall. Try to keep one hand free to hold the rail. Lamp cords and small rugs should be tacked down.

People often fall because they cannot see where they are going. Be sure that your halls are well lighted. Stairways should have a light switch that can be flicked from both the bottom and the top. All rooms should have a switch near the door so you can turn the light on without stumbling in the dark. There should be a night-light in the hallway, bedroom, and bathroom. These are some of the ways you can make a home safe for yourself and the baby.

Recalling Facts

1. Bad falls are the
   most common form of
   injury among
   ☐ a. young infants.
   ☐ b. middle-aged adults.
   ☐ c. teenagers.

2. Which of the following
   is the safest place to leave
   a child alone?
   ☐ a. a bed
   ☐ b. a couch
   ☐ c. a playpen

3. When a baby learns to crawl,
   you should block the
   ☐ a. bathroom.
   ☐ b. kitchen.
   ☐ c. stairways.

4. All rooms in a house should
   have a light switch near the
   ☐ a. door.
   ☐ b. floor.
   ☐ c. window.

5. For safety, a night-light should
   be placed in the
   ☐ a. den.
   ☐ b. hallways.
   ☐ c. kitchen.

Understanding the Passage

6. An infant can easily
   roll off a
   ☐ a. couch.
   ☐ b. crib.
   ☐ c. playpen.

7. A young tot is often
   ☐ a. careful.
   ☐ b. curious.
   ☐ c. still.

8. A good time to teach a
   child about danger is when
   the child begins to
   ☐ a. hear.
   ☐ b. talk.
   ☐ c. walk.

9. Many bad falls happen at
   ☐ a. home.
   ☐ b. parties.
   ☐ c. work.

10. This article tells us
    ☐ a. how to make our
          homes safer.
    ☐ b. why people use
          safety locks.
    ☐ c. when most accidents
          happen.

20

Grading of Eggs

The United States Department of Agriculture requires that a grade mark be used when labeling eggs. It is printed on the carton or on a tape used to seal the carton. It shows both the grade and the size of the eggs. Sometimes the size is not printed in the grade mark but is printed on the carton.

There are three grades for eggs. The top grade is U.S. Grade AA, or Fresh Fancy Quality. The next is U.S. Grade A. Grade B is the lowest grade. Some stores sell all three grades, and there may be quite a difference in price between the grades. The top two grades, AA and A, are best for frying and poaching. They don't spread out very much in the pan, and the yolk is not easily broken. Grade B eggs are just as good to eat. But the white is thinner. Also, the yolk may be flatter than in eggs of the higher grades. In most states, eggs marked with a grade and size must meet certain state laws. Many state's grade standards are the same as those of the U.S. government.

Eggs come in different sizes. But the size has nothing to do with the quality. The two decisions you must make when buying eggs are to choose the grade and the size. Eggs range in size from Jumbo to Pee Wee, and they are measured by their weight. A dozen Jumbo eggs must weigh a minimum of 30 ounces. A dozen Pee Wee eggs only needs to weigh 15 ounces.

Smaller eggs sell for less than bigger eggs because you buy them by weight just as you do other foods. For example, let's say Jumbo Grade A eggs are selling for $1.19 a dozen. To be of equal value, a dozen Large Grade A eggs would sell for about 20 cents less, or 99 cents. Medium Grade A eggs would sell for 9 cents less than the Larges, or 90 cents. If the smaller sizes were priced much below this, you could get more for your money by buying the smaller sizes.

A buyer should watch for bargains in these smaller-sized eggs in late summer and fall when they're plentiful. If a person makes it a habit to check the price difference between sizes, then it will be easy to spot the bargains when they're available. Comparison shopping will get you the most egg for the least money!

Recalling Facts

1. Which federal department requires grade marks on eggs?
   - ☐ a. Commerce
   - ☐ b. Interior
   - ☐ c. Agriculture

2. Grade marks indicate
   - ☐ a. size and quality.
   - ☐ b. color and texture.
   - ☐ c. price and shape.

3. The lowest grade allowed for eggs is
   - ☐ a. Grade B.
   - ☐ b. Grade C.
   - ☐ c. Grade D.

4. Grading marks are usually located on the
   - ☐ a. eggs.
   - ☐ b. carton.
   - ☐ c. receipt.

5. A dozen Pee Wee eggs need to weigh only
   - ☐ a. 10 ounces.
   - ☐ b. 15 ounces.
   - ☐ c. 30 ounces.

Understanding the Passage

6. When eggs are labeled Jumbo, we know that
   - ☐ a. this labeling is not legal.
   - ☐ b. these eggs would be bigger than Large.
   - ☐ c. no one would be able to afford these eggs.

7. A person who wishes to use eggs for poaching should buy
   - ☐ a. Grade B, Pee Wee.
   - ☐ b. Grade A, Large.
   - ☐ c. Grade B, Medium.

8. Which one of the following should be the most inexpensive
   - ☐ a. Grade AA, Medium
   - ☐ b. Grade A, Large
   - ☐ c. Grade B, Medium

9. U.S. Grade A eggs
   - ☐ a. have firm yolks.
   - ☐ b. are often smaller than other grades.
   - ☐ c. have thinner shells.

10. We can conclude that
   - ☐ a. supermarkets offer the lowest egg prices.
   - ☐ b. grade does not necessarily indicate price.
   - ☐ c. Medium and Large eggs are priced lower in winter.

21 Let's Solve That Problem Together

When a child is faced with a problem, he or she may not be able to deal with it. Children need to learn how. A puzzle piece may not fit, or an ice cream cone might fall on the ground. Then children turn to someone older for help. You can help someone to learn problem-solving skills. The best way is to take the time to talk about problems as they happen. Of course, this is not easy to do. Problems have a way of popping up at the worst times. But even if the time is not the best, you should try to help.

There are many things you can do to help a child learn problem-solving skills. One good way is to find out what caused the problem. This is a skill that children do not learn without help. A child may knock over his or her glass of milk at the dinner table, but he or she may not realize that the glass was too close to the edge. You can show the child what the problem is. Then it can be solved.

The next step for a child is to learn how to solve the problem alone. This step takes courage. Some people are so afraid of being wrong that they cannot solve problems. You can help by talking about some possible answers. The two of you can decide which answer is the best. Let the child try it out. Now the child will see that problems can be solved, and you can praise him or her for choosing an answer.

Another step to problem-solving is to help children see the laws of cause and effect. If a child knocks over a vase, it will fall and break. He or she might like to write on the wall. But the pencil always leaves a mark. Soon the child will see the link between cause and effect, and then he or she is on the road to growth. The child will see someone else knock over a vase. He or she now knows that it will break. The child may see writing on the wall. Now that child can tell how it got there.

The ability to solve problems is not easy for children to learn. It is not easy for adults either. It takes patience for you, and it takes practice for the child. But problem-solving can be taught. All you need is time and effort.

Recalling Facts

1. In order to teach problem-solving skills, you should take the time to talk about problems
   - ☐ a. before they happen.
   - ☐ b. as they happen.
   - ☐ c. after they happen.

2. One way to help a youngster solve a problem is to
   - ☐ a. find out the cause.
   - ☐ b. forget the problem.
   - ☐ c. punish the child.

3. In order for a child to choose a solution, he needs
   - ☐ a. courage.
   - ☐ b. honesty.
   - ☐ c. talent.

4. One step to problem-solving is to help the youngster see the laws of
   - ☐ a. cause and effect.
   - ☐ b. space and distance.
   - ☐ c. time and sequence.

5. Problem-solving is a skill that can be
   - ☐ a. forgotten.
   - ☐ b. ignored.
   - ☐ c. learned.

Understanding the Passage

6. The writer makes this article clear by using
   - ☐ a. examples.
   - ☐ b. graphs.
   - ☐ c. numbers.

7. Problem-solving is not
   - ☐ a. easy.
   - ☐ b. a skill.
   - ☐ c. taught.

8. This article suggests that
   - ☐ a. anyone can learn to solve problems.
   - ☐ b. children can easily solve their own problems.
   - ☐ c. most problems cannot be solved.

9. When an adult and a child try to choose a solution to a problem, they should
   - ☐ a. begin by discussing the different solutions.
   - ☐ b. disagree about its solutions.
   - ☐ c. try to find out who is to blame.

10. According to this article,
    - ☐ a. it takes practice and patience to solve problems.
    - ☐ b. people often make their own problems.
    - ☐ c. the problems that occur daily are easy to solve.

22   Probing with a Purpose

NASA's space science program is yielding a wealth of knowledge. In the summer of 1977, NASA launched two Voyager probes. They are now on their endless journey through space. On their way, the probes will explore the planets. The probes' path leads by Jupiter, Saturn, and perhaps Uranus. The crafts will then whirl through space. They may travel for millions of years.

The Voyager program is a big help to NASA. It gives NASA a close look at the planets. From the Voyager's flight, new facts can be found. The questions of the birth and life of the solar system may now soon be solved. ●

Studying the planets is only one part of a carefully planned space science program. NASA is also studying Earth, its moon, and its atmosphere. Studying our sun and the stars of our galaxy are other goals of the program. In life research, we hope to gain knowledge of the effect that space has on living things. Some of the tools of this great project are the deep-space probes and the satellites. Other tools that NASA uses are rockets, aircraft, and balloons. Such things as radio telescopes are also used in this study.

The purpose behind these probes and searches is the same as that of ● all research—to help people. In space science, the benefits may not be seen right away. Still, they are vital to the future of us all. Today's scientists might not be able to find a use for all of the knowledge gained in the space science program. Still, what we learn now may be useful someday. As we learn more and more about our world, pieces of the puzzle will begin to fit together. Future scientists may find uses for this knowledge that will benefit our grandchildren.

All of NASA's space science program share a common end. They all ● want to learn more about Earth. Only by exploring other bodies in the skies can we answer some of the questions we have about Earth. The things we have learned about other planets have helped us to know our own planet better. It is important to understand the forces that control Earth. With that knowledge we may be able to manage those forces. This control will help us. It will help to improve our lives. It will give our children a better world in which to live.

Recalling Facts

1. NASA's space science program is giving us a lot of —
   - ☐ a. knowledge.
   - ☐ b. talent.
   - ☐ c. trouble.

2. In what year were the Voyager probes launched?
   - ☐ a. 1975
   - ☐ b. 1976
   - ☐ c. 1977

3. Which of the following planets will the Voyagers pass?
   - ☐ a. Jupiter
   - ☐ b. Neptune
   - ☐ c. Pluto

4. NASA is also interested in the Earth's moon and the Earth's
   - ☐ a. atmosphere.
   - ☐ b. mountains.
   - ☐ c. oceans.

5. In order to gain information about the planets, NASA uses deep-space probes and
   - ☐ a. comets.
   - ☐ b. meteors.
   - ☐ c. satellites.

Understanding the Passage

6. Which of these would be a good title for the article?
   - ☐ a. How to Build a Spaceship
   - ☐ b. NASA's Space Science Program
   - ☐ c. Visitors from Outer Space

7. After the probes pass Jupiter, Saturn, and Uranus, they will
   - ☐ a. burn up.
   - ☐ b. keep on going.
   - ☐ c. return to Earth.

8. The Voyager program gives us knowledge of other
   - ☐ a. people.
   - ☐ b. planets.
   - ☐ c. religions.

9. The goal of all research is to
   - ☐ a. detect life on other planets.
   - ☐ b. make things better for man.
   - ☐ c. stop war before it starts.

10. This article hints that some knowledge cannot be used right away, so it is
    - ☐ a. completely forgotten.
    - ☐ b. kept for later use.
    - ☐ c. ignored and destroyed.

23 In Praise of Trees

Have you ever thought of a tree as being a good friend? A tree can give us much in the way of shelter, warmth, fun, and even learning. We also look for these things in our friends. Read further to see how a tree provides all these things.

When a tree is first planted, its growth is rapid. Over months and years the trunk will become thicker. Branches and limbs will sprout from the trunk. Birds use these branches for their nests. This is where their young first learn about the world. Squirrels also call a tree home. They can be seen scurrying up a trunk storing acorns for the winter.

We can learn about the seasons from a tree. With spring's arrival, many trees are adorned with beautiful blossoms. Crab, cherry, apple, and lilac trees all have colorful blossoms. Lush green leaves of summer show vibrant colors during the fall. In the winter, trees with bare limbs stretch up to the gray sky.

The trunk of a tree is a great place to lean back and enjoy a good book. Or, if you want to do some climbing, the branches of a tree provide a ladder to the sky. On a warm day, the grand leaves of an oak offer pleasant shade. Sometimes the leaves of a tree act like an umbrella to protect you during a rainstorm.

Dead branches are good fuel for a roaring evening campfire. Many people are thankful for the needed warmth that wood from the forests provides them during the cold winter months. In years past, burning wood for fuel was the standard way to heat homes.

Trees provide lumber that builds many items. Houses are made with lumber from various types of trees. Many buildings contain some type of wood in their structures. Wood is used as decoration both inside and outside. Wood is used to build items we use for recreation. Most picnic tables and rowboats are built with wood. Objects can be carved from small blocks of wood. Craftsmen make detailed furniture from wood.

Trees fill countless needs in our daily lives. They give us pleasure. Their colorful leaves in fall are beautiful. They provide necessities. Paper we write on comes from trees.

To protect trees as a natural resource, we must plant new trees each year. New trees will replace the ones we cut down. Care must be taken to help them thrive.

Recalling Facts

1. A tree provides the same
   things that
   - ☐ a. a friend does.
   - ☐ b. nature can.
   - ☐ c. a ranger could.

2. Birds use the branches of
   a tree for
   - ☐ a. their nests.
   - ☐ b. finding worms.
   - ☐ c. storing acorns.

3. Wood from trees provide
   fuel for
   - ☐ a. swinging.
   - ☐ b. building.
   - ☐ c. fires.

4. Which tree has colorful
   blossoms?
   - ☐ a. elm
   - ☐ b. lilac
   - ☐ c. oak

5. Protecting trees as a natural
   resource means
   - ☐ a. putting "No Trespassing"
     signs near tree farms.
   - ☐ b. maintaining full-time
     forest rangers.
   - ☐ c. planting new trees
     to replace the ones
     cut down.

Understanding the Passage

6. Squirrels use hollow trees for
   - ☐ a. homes and food storage.
   - ☐ b. lumber for nests.
   - ☐ c. food and fires.

7. The leaves on a tree tell
   us about the
   - ☐ a. different seasons.
   - ☐ b. kind of bird living in a tree.
   - ☐ c. age of a tree.

8. A tree can be like an umbrella in
   the rain because its
   - ☐ a. roots are large.
   - ☐ b. branches never break.
   - ☐ c. leaves provide shelter.

9. Reading would be difficult
   without
   - ☐ a. colorful leaves.
   - ☐ b. paper from trees.
   - ☐ c. blocks of lumber.

10. Today, most people receive
    heat from
    - ☐ a. something other than wood.
    - ☐ b. mostly wood.
    - ☐ c. a combination of wood
      and coal.

A Word to the Wise

The first step in wise car care and service is to buy a car that is in perfect condition. Look the car over carefully to make sure that it doesn't have any built-in flaws or service headaches. Be sure you know how to operate your car. Sit in the driver's seat and have the salesman explain how to start the car. He will show you the gauges and the warning lights. He will also point out the knobs and controls. Make sure you learn the location of all of the controls. Read the warranty well and note the services that are free. Find those that you must pay for. Be aware that the new car warranty will not pay for normal wear or abuse. You must pay these costs yourself.

Check the outside of the car. Look for dents or scratches in the paint. Check inside the car, too. Look at the seats. See if there are tears, scuffs, or crooked seams. Check the door panels and headlining for these same flaws. Do the rug and floor mats fit well? Open and close the car doors two or three times. Do the doors fit the frames? Do they close completely? Roll the windows up and down. Do they work smoothly and close all the way? Have the salesman try all the lights and turn signals while you stand outside the car to make sure they work.

Look in the trunk for the spare tire. Find the tire jack and lug wrench; make sure they are there. Ask the salesman to show you how the jack works. Look under the hood at the engine. Is it new and clean? Ask how to check the oil level and other fluids. Start the engine and listen for any noise. The car should run smoothly after it has warmed up. If the car has an automatic transmission, step on the brake and shift to "drive." The engine should run without stalling. All these simple things should be checked before you leave the dealer's lot.

Next, road test the car. It should speed up without jerking, and the brakes should work evenly and quickly. The steering should be smooth and sure. Try the horn and the windshield wipers and washer.

If the car fails to perform on any of these points, do not take it. Insist that the faults be fixed before you accept it.

Recalling Facts

1. The first step in wise car care and service is to buy a car that is
   - ☐ a. bright and shiny.
   - ☐ b. in good running condition.
   - ☐ c. old enough to be experienced.

2. Some free services are covered under the
   - ☐ a. contract.
   - ☐ b. insurance.
   - ☐ c. warranty.

3. When checking the outside of the car, you should look for
   - ☐ a. spare tires.
   - ☐ b. dents or scratches.
   - ☐ c. the license plate.

4. The trunk of the car should contain
   - ☐ a. an extra set of tools.
   - ☐ b. a list of recent repairs.
   - ☐ c. a spare tire and jack.

5. The engine of a car should run
   - ☐ a. noisily.
   - ☐ b. roughly.
   - ☐ c. smoothly.

Understanding the Passage

6. What is this article about?
   - ☐ a. repairing old cars
   - ☐ b. visiting a used car lot
   - ☐ c. selecting a good car

7. A warranty provides
   - ☐ a. extra parts for your car.
   - ☐ b. services you don't have to pay for.
   - ☐ c. road maps and toll tokens.

8. It is important to check the engine to make sure it
   - ☐ a. has been painted.
   - ☐ b. is well placed.
   - ☐ c. runs well.

9. After you have looked a car over on the lot, you should
   - ☐ a. buy it.
   - ☐ b. test drive it.
   - ☐ c. wash it.

10. Sometimes, before you buy a car, it has to be
    - ☐ a. borrowed.
    - ☐ b. licensed.
    - ☐ c. repaired.

25 Go West!

Imagine you and your family live in a bustling New England town during the 1800s. Your father works as a blacksmith. He has heard stories of an exciting land out west. Your father decides to try his luck in this new land. You begin to help your family prepare for the long trip.

Your father buys a wagon pulled by a team of horses. This will be your family's home for many months. It will be part of a large wagon train. Other families will also be going west. You help your brothers and sisters pack belongings in a huge trunk. Your mother stores boxes and sacks of food and supplies in the wagon.

When it is time to leave, the wagons start off in a long line. Several men ride on horseback. They circle the wagons to watch for breakdowns. Some men also ride ahead to check for clear trails. At the beginning of the trip you sit up at the front of the wagon. You want to see everything. Later, you go inside the wagon and try to rest. It is very hard to sleep because of the bouncing wagon.

At night, the wagons stop and form a wide circle. This is to protect the people and horses from wild animals. You have also heard the men talk about Indians. You hope you have a chance to meet some. After a supper of beans and rabbit stew, you wander through the camp. A group of men is singing cowboy songs. You fall asleep to the music under a starlit sky.

In the morning, the wagon train stops by a small pond. The horses are in need of a long drink of water. Many people decide to swim or wash clothing. It is not known when water will be found again. Suddenly, a loud whoop is heard. Everyone rushes back to the wagons. They are surrounded by Indians! The men drop their guns to show they don't want to fight. The head of the wagon train steps forward. He points to the wagons and then to the trail. The chief points to the water and to the other Indians. After a while, the Indians understand that the travelers are not here to take their water supply. Everyone shakes hands. The Indians ride away. You find a bright feather from the chief's headdress. What an adventure this trip will be!

Recalling Facts

1. The form of vehicle used to go West in was a
   - ☐ a. bicycle.
   - ☐ b. wagon.
   - ☐ c. ferry.

2. The wagons formed a circle around the campfire
   - ☐ a. to keep wild animals out.
   - ☐ b. because the food cooked more quickly.
   - ☐ c. so that their singing wouldn't be heard.

3. The men on horseback were
   - ☐ a. fighting Indians.
   - ☐ b. pulling wagons.
   - ☐ c. watching for breakdowns.

4. The father in the story worked as a
   - ☐ a. blacksmith.
   - ☐ b. barber.
   - ☐ c. banker.

5. The men dropped their guns to
   - ☐ a. surrender to the Indians.
   - ☐ b. show they didn't want to fight.
   - ☐ c. trick the Indians.

Understanding the Passage

6. Families went west because they
   - ☐ a. were out of work.
   - ☐ b. were driven from their land.
   - ☐ c. wanted to start a new life.

7. For entertainment on the trip, people
   - ☐ a. sang songs.
   - ☐ b. washed clothes.
   - ☐ c. rode horses.

8. Finding water was important because it
   - ☐ a. helped the travelers meet Indians.
   - ☐ b. gave the travelers a chance to go swimming.
   - ☐ c. could be a while before water was found again.

9. To understand each other, the wagon train leader and the Indian chief
   - ☐ a. didn't have to speak the same language.
   - ☐ b. threw water at each other.
   - ☐ c. showed each other how to ride horses.

10. It is not easy to sleep in a moving wagon because
   - ☐ a. there are too many people inside.
   - ☐ b. the ride is very bumpy.
   - ☐ c. there aren't any beds.

Painting can be done with a brush, a roller, or a spray gun. A brush helps to get paint into pores and cracks. Brushing is often the best way to apply prime coats and outside paints.

When you buy a brush, you should choose one that is wide enough. A wide brush will cover the most area in the least time. If you have to paint a large area like a wall or floor, you will want to use a brush that is four or five inches wide. If you have to paint windows or trim, your brush should be narrow. For such narrow surfaces, you should use a brush that is one or one-and-a-half inches wide. The bristles on a good brush are long and thick. This lets the brush hold a good amount of paint. The bristles should bend easily, too. This lets you use smooth and even strokes. If you paint only once in a while, you do not need an expensive brush. A medium-priced one will do the job well.

Paint should first be brushed up and down. Then, use cross strokes to get the paint on evenly. If you are painting a rough surface, keep changing the strokes. This method helps the paint to sink in well. When you paint, hold the brush at a slight angle. Do not use too much pressure. If you force the brush into cracks and corners, you can hurt the bristles. Always start to paint at the top and then move down. In the house, do ceilings and walls first. Then do doors, windows, and trim. If floors are to be painted, they should be done last. Always work toward the wet edge of the part just painted. Do not try to cover too large a surface with each brush load.

If you buy a good brush, it pays to take the time and effort to take proper care of it. Clean the brush right after painting. Use a paint thinner or a brush cleaner. Your hardware store can advise you on what to use. Latex paints, for example, can be cleaned from brushes with just soap and water. If any paint is allowed to dry on a brush, you will need to use a paint remover or brush-cleaning solvent.

If you take proper care of your paintbrush, it will give you years of excellent service.

Recalling Facts

1. Painting can be done with a brush, a roller, or a
   - ☐ a. garden hose.
   - ☐ b. hollow tube.
   - ☐ c. spray gun.

2. A brush that is four inches wide is used to paint
   - ☐ a. trim.
   - ☐ b. walls.
   - ☐ c. windows.

3. The bristles on a good brush should be
   - ☐ a. fat and short.
   - ☐ b. long and thick.
   - ☐ c. short and thin.

4. When painting an entire room, the floor should be done
   - ☐ a. first.
   - ☐ b. second.
   - ☐ c. last.

5. Latex paint can be cleaned from brushes by using
   - ☐ a. gasoline.
   - ☐ b. linseed oil.
   - ☐ c. soap and water.

Understanding the Passage

6. Prime coats should be applied with a
   - ☐ a. brush.
   - ☐ b. roller.
   - ☐ c. sponge.

7. The brush you use to paint windows should be about
   - ☐ a. one-and-one half inches wide.
   - ☐ b. four or five inches wide.
   - ☐ c. six-and-one-half inches wide.

8. A thick paintbrush
   - ☐ a. has a short handle.
   - ☐ b. holds a lot of paint.
   - ☐ c. is easy to clean.

9. One of the first things you should do as soon as you finish painting is
   - ☐ a. clean your brush.
   - ☐ b. scrape the floor.
   - ☐ c. wash your clothes.

10. If you clean a paintbrush properly, it will
    - ☐ a. become stiff and hard.
    - ☐ b. fall apart.
    - ☐ c. last a long time.

Cold Weather Care

Enjoy the great outdoors, but be careful. People who are outside when it is very cold and windy tire quickly. Also, body heat is lost rapidly. If you must go outdoors, take extra care. Cold weather itself, without any work on your part, puts an extra strain on the heart. If you add to this the strain of hard work, you are taking a risk. Hard work includes shoveling snow, pushing a stalled car, or even just walking too fast or too far.

If you do go out, be sure to dress warmly. Try to wear light wool clothes that do not fit too tightly. Outer garments should shed water. Wear a wool hat. Protect your face and cover your mouth to keep very cold air from your lungs. Wear mittens instead of gloves. They allow your fingers to move freely and will keep your hands warmer.

Watch out for frostbite and any other signs of danger from being in the cold too long. Frostbite causes a loss of feeling in the fingers, toes, tip of the nose, or ear lobes. These areas may become white or pale. If you see such signs, get help right away. Do not rub them with snow or ice. This treatment does not help and could make matters worse.

Do not drink alcohol when you are out in the cold. This makes you lose body heat even faster. You may feel warmer at first, but you will end up colder than before.

Try to keep your clothes and yourself dry. Change wet socks right away. To stop loss of body heat, remove all wet clothing as soon as you can. Wet clothes do not help you to keep in body heat.

If someone with you shows signs of illness from the cold, take action quickly. Even if someone claims to be all right, you should still act. Often the person will not realize how bad the situation may be. Get the person into dry clothing and a warm bed. Use a hot water bottle which should not be hot but warm to the touch. Use warm towels or a heating pad or any other source of heat to warm the bed. Put the heat on the person's trunk first. Keep the person's head low and his feet up. Give the person warm drinks. If symptoms are very bad, call for a doctor right away.

Recalling Facts

1. People who go outside in very cold windy weather usually
   - ☐ a. die.
   - ☐ b. get lost.
   - ☐ c. tire quickly.

2. Cold weather puts an extra strain on the
   - ☐ a. brain.
   - ☐ b. heart.
   - ☐ c. kidneys.

3. In cold weather, the face and mouth should be protected to keep cold air from the
   - ☐ a. eyes.
   - ☐ b. lungs.
   - ☐ c. throat.

4. Frostbite causes a loss of
   - ☐ a. feeling.
   - ☐ b. memory.
   - ☐ c. speech.

5. Alcohol makes you lose
   - ☐ a. added weight.
   - ☐ b. body heat.
   - ☐ c. extra water.

Understanding the Passage

6. Being out in very cold weather can be
   - ☐ a. dangerous.
   - ☐ b. fun.
   - ☐ c. helpful.

7. This article hints that
   - ☐ a. alcohol warms the blood.
   - ☐ b. wet clothes keep the body warm.
   - ☐ c. wool clothes are warm.

8. We can see that frostbite
   - ☐ a. does not require immediate attention.
   - ☐ b. makes the skin very white.
   - ☐ c. puts an extra strain on the heart.

9. If someone shows signs of illness from the cold, you should
   - ☐ a. get the person to drink some alcohol.
   - ☐ b. rub the person with snow or ice.
   - ☐ c. try to keep the person warm.

10. Which of these would be a good title for this article?
    - ☐ a. How to Handle Cold Weather
    - ☐ b. Old Wives' Tales
    - ☐ c. Weather Patterns of the United States

28 Clothing Makes the Difference

There are many ways to learn about people of other lands. Some of these ways can be fun. One way is to study the clothing other people wear.

For thousands of years, people in different parts of the world have worn very different types of clothing. There are four big reasons for this.

First, there are different reasons for wearing clothes. One reason is to protect the body against the weather. Another reason might be religion. In many Moslem countries, women must wear veils to hide their faces. The veils must be worn in public. Veils are part of the Moslem religion.

A second reason for the difference in clothing the world over is that different materials are used in different countries. For instance, in France the fabrics used in clothing may be cotton, fur, leather, silk, wool, or many of the man-made materials. Most people in China wear cotton. Studying the type of material may give you some idea about the people of a distant land.

The way clothes are made varies from country to country. This is another reason why people dress differently. Western countries rely on machines to make most of their clothing. Someone living in India can use only hand power to make the fabric and the clothing he needs.

Worldwide differences in customs also lead to differences in clothing. Customs vary from continent to continent and from country to country. Let's look at clothing customs and how they can affect the style of dress. A Mexican farmer wears a straw hat with a brim that tilts up. In China, a farmer wears a straw hat with a brim that tilts down. Both hats are used to protect the farmer from the sun. The difference is the custom of each country. Some of these customs have come down through thousands of years.

Right now, the clothing industry is very large. It includes jewelry and shoes. It also includes buttons, hooks and eyes, snaps, zippers, and threads. It includes clothes for men, women, children, and infants. America leads the world in the clothing industry. Russia is second. Some main clothing spots in the world are London, New York City, Paris, and Rome. These cities are also the big fashion spots. They set the trend for cities around the world.

Recalling Facts

1. People wear clothes to
   - ☐ a. be colorful.
   - ☐ b. protect themselves.
   - ☑ c. show their wealth.

2. Moslem women cover their faces with a
   - ☐ a. bandage.
   - ☐ b. hat.
   - ☑ c. veil.

3. Which fabric do most people in China wear?
   - ☐ a. cotton
   - ☐ b. nylon
   - ☐ c. silk

4. Which country leads the world in the clothing industry?
   - ☑ a. America
   - ☐ b. France
   - ☐ c. Italy

5. Which city is a big fashion center?
   - ☐ a. Miami
   - ☐ b. Naples
   - ☑ c. Paris

Understanding the Passage

6. What is the main idea of this article?
   - ☐ a. Moslem countries use a lot of silk.
   - ☑ b. People dress differently all around the world.
   - ☐ c. Russia is the world's biggest fashion center.

7. This article hints that Moslem women cannot
   - ☐ a. get a job.
   - ☐ b. go out alone.
   - ☑ c. reveal their faces.

8. People in France wear a lot of
   - ☐ a. jewelry.
   - ☑ b. man-made fabrics.
   - ☐ c. soft material.

9. Most western clothes are made in
   - ☑ a. factories.
   - ☐ b. homes.
   - ☐ c. stores.

10. This article hints that
    - ☐ a. America makes a lot of clothes.
    - ☐ b. many people like to wear furs.
    - ☐ c. Russian clothes are not very heavy.

29   Caves

Underground caves are exciting places to visit. Exploring a cave allows you to get a different view of the earth—the view underground! A cave is a hollow area in the earth. It is large enough for a person to enter. Some caves consist of just a single chamber. Others are vast networks of passages and chambers.

The inside of a cave is completely dark. With artificial light, a strange underground landscape is seen. A cave may have lakes, rivers, or waterfalls. Odd-shaped rocks called speleothems loom inside.

Speleothems are formed by drops of water containing minerals. When water seeps into a cave, the minerals may crystallize. These crystal deposits build up to form speleothems. The best-known kinds of speleothems are stalactites and stalagmites. Stalactites look like icicles. They hang from the cave's ceiling. Stalagmites are pillars that rise from the floor. These two kinds of speleothems may join to form a column.

To view the inside of caves many people take up cave exploration, or "spelunking." Spelunking can be rather dangerous. A person should never go into a cave alone. An experienced spelunker should lead any group that is exploring a cave.

Like mountain climbing, spelunking requires proper equipment. Ropes and ladders should be used. Hardhats and heavy clothing are necessary. These will protect you from the sharp rocks which could cause injury, and from dripping water. Spelunkers should carry two sources of light. You should carry a flashlight. And a headlamp should be attached to your hardhat.

An important part of spelunking is to leave the cave as it is found. Don't leave trash or food in the cave. Be careful when touching speleothems. They are fragile and impossible to restore if broken or damaged. Try not to disturb the animal life in the cave. Well-known animals such as bears and bats sometimes live in caves. But there are also some very rare animals called troglobites in caves. Troglobites include certain kinds of beetles, spiders, and fish. They live in the darkest parts of most caves. There is no light or wind here. Most troglobites are blind and must rely on highly developed senses of smell and touch to survive.

Some caves have been explored many times. These may be open for tourists. There are well-lighted paths to walk on and displays to explain formations. These tourist attractions are good practice ground for a beginning spelunker.

Recalling Facts

1. A cave is a
   - ☐ a. man-made tunnel.
   - ☐ b. hollow place in the earth.
   - ☐ c. natural formation near water.

2. The unusual rocks inside a cave are formed by
   - ☐ a. crystallized minerals.
   - ☐ b. stagnant water.
   - ☐ c. clay deposits.

3. Cave exploring is also called
   - ☐ a. hiking.
   - ☐ b. spelunking.
   - ☐ c. stalagmiting.

4. A person exploring a cave should always
   - ☐ a. take along a detailed map.
   - ☐ b. carry two types of hardhats.
   - ☐ c. carry two sources of light.

5. Very rare animals living in caves are
   - ☐ a. troglobites.
   - ☐ b. stalactites.
   - ☐ c. bears.

Understanding the Passage

6. Without artificial light, it would be
   - ☐ a. possible to see the inside of the cave.
   - ☐ b. impossible to see the inside of the cave.
   - ☐ c. easy to tell your location inside of the cave.

7. Speleothems cannot be
   - ☐ a. replaced.
   - ☐ b. broken.
   - ☐ c. reused.

8. Some speleothem formations may look like
   - ☐ a. waving flags.
   - ☐ b. small clay sculptures.
   - ☐ c. columns or pillars.

9. Most spelunkers are concerned about
   - ☐ a. electric lighting in caves.
   - ☐ b. pollution in caves.
   - ☐ c. wide paths in caves.

10. A person's first spelunking adventure should probably take place in a
    - ☐ a. cave with paths and displays.
    - ☐ b. museum devoted to cave explorations.
    - ☐ c. book dealing with hiking.

Save the Model A

Between 1927 and 1932, the Ford Motor Company built some 5 million Model A cars. Nearly 250,000 are still being used. They can be seen chugging along the highways. The number could even be growing. Thousands of the old cars are being saved from the scrap heaps. They are being fixed. Many are in good-as-new condition.

Why the Model A? What made it so unlike all the other cars that have dropped from sight? In one word, the answer is simplicity. With a few tools, almost anyone could fix this car.

But how did this car come about? The easy-to-fix Model A was the work of Henry Ford himself. At first he did not want to build the car. He wanted to stick to building the Model T. The Model T had sold for nearly 20 years without a change in its design. But then Henry's son convinced him that people wanted style in their cars. Henry gave in. Soon the designing of the Model A began. Mr. Ford, however, examined each one of the auto's 5,500 parts. He allowed the Model A to have a modern look. Still, he kept some of the simple ideas found in the old Model T.

The Model A sold for about $500. Its design made the car one of the hottest things on the road. It had many of the things found in today's sports cars: crash gear box, quick cornering, ease of handling, rapid start-up. Some of the Ford's parts were so good that they were used for years. Orders for the new Model A cars were placed faster than they could be filled. Dealers across the land hadn't even seen the car. They were selling hundreds just from photographs of the car. The orders kept rolling in.

When production finally caught up with sales, Model As of all sorts were built. They were not just family cars. There were taxis with a glass window between the front and rear seats. A town car was built with an enclosed back seat and an open seat for the hired driver. The car could also be used in other ways. Special wheels were used to turn the car into a farm tractor. Saw rigs, pumps, generating plants, and many other pieces of farm equipment could also be powered by the A's engine. The Model A was a car with many uses.

Recalling Facts

1. How many Model A cars did the Ford Motor Company build between 1927 and 1932?
   - ☐ a. 2 million
   - ☐ b. 3 million
   - ☐ c. 5 million

2. About how many Model A cars travel the highways today?
   - ☐ a. 100,000
   - ☐ b. 250,000
   - ☐ c. 500,000

3. Who invented the Model A?
   - ☐ a. Charles Darwin
   - ☐ b. Henry Ford
   - ☐ c. Robert Browning

4. The first Model A cars sold for about
   - ☐ a. $100.
   - ☐ b. $200.
   - ☐ c. $500.

5. Special wheels were used to turn the Model A into a
   - ☐ a. plow.
   - ☐ b. motorcycle.
   - ☐ c. tractor.

Understanding the Passage

6. The Model A was popular because it was
   - ☐ a. easy to fix.
   - ☐ b. pretty to look at.
   - ☐ c. very expensive.

7. For 20 years the Motel T didn't change its
   - ☐ a. color.
   - ☐ b. name.
   - ☐ c. shape.

8. The Model A was built
   - ☐ a. before the Model T.
   - ☐ b. at the same time as the Model T.
   - ☐ c. after the Model T.

9. Some people bought the Model A
   - ☐ a. because they were rich.
   - ☐ b. to use as a show piece.
   - ☐ c. without actually seeing it.

10. This article suggests that the Model A
    - ☐ a. could be used for many things.
    - ☐ b. never became very popular.
    - ☐ c. was an expensive car to run.

31 A Day To Be Thankful

The first Thanksgiving Day celebration in America was in the fall of 1621. The colonists gathered to give thanks for the summer's harvest. They had struggled through a hard winter. Many people had died. The cold was terrible. There had not been much food that first winter.

These colonists were also celebrating life in the new land. They had sailed from England the year before. Now they faced new challenges. But the most important thing to do was to make sure there was enough food. Building shelters was also important.

After landing here, the colonists learned that they weren't alone. Indians also had their homes in the new land. Although they lived differently, the Indians and the colonists became friends. The Indians taught the colonists how to plant. They also taught them how to hunt.

At the first Thanksgiving, the colonists celebrated with the Indians. The women of the colony spent days fixing the feast. Children turned roasts on spits. Indians brought wild turkeys and deer meat. The men of the colony brought geese, ducks, and fish. Everyone ate outdoors at big tables.

The Thanksgiving feast did not take place each year. In following years, different towns celebrated for many reasons. The gatherings weren't always held in the fall. Sometimes people would meet to give thanks for rain or for good crops. They might meet to help build a house or to celebrate a marriage.

On Thursday, November 26, 1789, the first national Thanksgiving was observed. This wasn't just to give thanks for a good supply of food. President Washington called this day to honor the forming of the Constitution of the United States. Even after this announcement, Thanksgiving was not always observed.

In 1863, President Lincoln began the regular practice of a Thanksgiving Day. He set the last Thursday in November as a day to give thanks. This was during the Civil War. He felt it was good to give thanks even though the country was in hard times. Lincoln's choice to have a day of Thanksgiving was not all his own. It was also in response to Mrs. Sara Josepha Hale. She had worked for years to have a national Thanksgiving Day.

Each year since 1863, the President of the United States has supported the national holiday. Most families have their own traditions. The idea of giving thanks is still important to them.

Recalling Facts

1. America's first Thanksgiving
   Day celebration was in
   - ☐ a. 1621.
   - ☐ b. 1701.
   - ☐ c. 1821.

2. The colonists were friendly
   with the
   - ☐ a. French.
   - ☐ b. British.
   - ☐ c. Indians.

3. President Washington
   observed Thanksgiving Day
   - ☐ a. to honor the Constitution.
   - ☐ b. to give thanks for food.
   - ☐ c. during the Civil War.

4. Lincoln's decision to celebrate
   Thanksgiving Day was partly
   due to
   - ☐ a. the Indians.
   - ☐ b. Mrs. Sara Josepha Hale.
   - ☐ c. the Revolutionary War.

5. On the first Thanksgiving
   celebration, colonists
   shared their
   - ☐ a. homes.
   - ☐ b. food.
   - ☐ c. clothing.

Understanding the Passage

6. When they arrived in the new
   land, the colonists
   - ☐ a. kept in close contact with
     relatives in England.
   - ☐ b. were not prepared for their
     first winter.
   - ☐ c. were terribly frightened of
     the Indians.

7. The first Thanksgiving Day meal
   - ☐ a. consisted mostly of corn.
   - ☐ b. saddened the colonists.
   - ☐ c. required much preparation.

8. Even during hard times, people
   found reasons to
   - ☐ a. build homes.
   - ☐ b. be thankful.
   - ☐ c. eat a lot of food.

9. Celebrating a national
   Thanksgiving Day seemed to
   - ☐ a. be a simple event to
     establish.
   - ☐ b. not be widely accepted
     at first.
   - ☐ c. create problems in Congress.

10. Over the years, Americans have
    given thanks
    - ☐ a. only on Thanksgiving Day.
    - ☐ b. for many different reasons.
    - ☐ c. practically never.

32 A Pressing Choice

Modern electric irons have made ironing and pressing clothes an easy job. But there are a few things you should know about different kinds of irons. Then you can choose the iron that best suits your needs.

The dry iron is simple. It is cheap. Its only working parts are a heating element, a thermostat, and a temperature setting. It is mainly used on heavy, dampened cloth. On the other hand, steam and steam/spray irons are used for many different jobs.

The steam/spray iron has a nozzle that sprays water to help remove wrinkles. With the steam on, it can touch up permanent press clothes. It can raise the nap on velvets and corduroys. And it can block knits or press wools. With the steam off, it can be used as a dry iron.

The dry iron, the steam, and the steam/spray iron are all rather bulky. However, the travel iron is small and light. It has a handle that folds. It can be easily packed into a suitcase. Some travel irons also have steam or steam/spray features.

After you decide upon the type of iron you want, there are other things you should check. The controls on an iron should be well marked and easy to work. Grasp the handle of the iron you like. Hold it in the ironing position. If you must shift your grasp to see or use the controls, the iron will be difficult to use. Try another brand or style.

The heel rest, which may be the back of the handle or a handle with crosspieces, should be strong. The iron should not tip easily when in the rest, or upright position. As a test, place the iron upright. Next, push gently against the top. If the iron falls easily then you may want to choose another.

Another thing to look at is the electrical cord on the iron. Check to make sure that the cord is well placed, so that you can iron with either hand on either side of the ironing board. Some irons have cords that can be moved from one side of the handle to the other. On other irons the cords cannot be moved. You must decide which is best for you. Choose your iron with care, and you will be sure to purchase the one most suitable for the type of ironing you do.

Recalling Facts

1. How many working parts does the dry iron have?
   - ☐ a. one
   - ☐ b. two
   - ☐ c. three

2. The dry iron is mostly used on
   - ☐ a. fine, silk cloth.
   - ☐ b. heavy, dampened cloth.
   - ☐ c. permanent press cloth.

3. Steam irons can raise the nap on
   - ☐ a. cotton.
   - ☐ b. silk.
   - ☐ c. velvet.

4. A steam/spray iron has a special nozzle that sprays
   - ☐ a. bleach.
   - ☐ b. starch.
   - ☐ c. water.

5. The travel iron is small and
   - ☐ a. bulky.
   - ☐ b. colorful.
   - ☐ c. light.

Understanding the Passage

6. Electric irons make ironing
   - ☐ a. difficult.
   - ☐ b. easy.
   - ☐ c. hard.

7. This article suggests that
   - ☐ a. ironing clothes is a difficult job.
   - ☐ b. some people do not like to iron.
   - ☐ c. some irons have more than one use.

8. Steam irons can also be used as
   - ☐ a. branding irons.
   - ☐ b. dry irons.
   - ☐ c. flat irons.

9. You can remove wrinkles from cloth by
   - ☐ a. folding it in a towel.
   - ☐ b. washing it in bleach and water.
   - ☐ c. wetting and then ironing it.

10. A good heel rest is
    - ☐ a. firm.
    - ☐ b. pretty.
    - ☐ c. unsteady.

To help ourselves and others, it is important to know something about drugs. A drug is a chemical substance. It can bring about a physical, emotional, or mental change in people. Alcohol and tobacco are drugs. The caffeine found in coffee, tea, cocoa, and some soft drinks is a drug.

Drug abuse is the use of a drug, legal or illegal, that hurts a person or someone close to him. A drug user is the person who takes the drug. There are many kinds of drug users. There are experimental users. These people may try drugs once or twice. They want to see what the effects will be. ●
Recreational users take drugs to get high. They use drugs with friends or at parties to get into the mood of things. Regular users take drugs all the time. But they are often able to keep up with the normal routine of work, school, housework, and so on. Dependent users can't relate to anything but drugs. Their whole life centers around drugs. They feel extreme mental or physical pain when without drugs.

All drugs can be harmful. The effect of any drug depends on a lot of things. How a drug acts depends on how much or how often it is taken. ●
It depends on the way it is taken. Some drugs are smoked. Others are swallowed or injected. Drugs act differently on different people. The place and the people around you affect the way a drug works.

Sometimes people take more than one drug. Multiple drug use is not only common, but also harmful. A deadly example is the use of alcohol and sleeping pills at the same time. Together these drugs can stop normal breathing and lead to death.

It is not always easy to tell if someone is using drugs. In the early stages, ●
drug use is often hard to see. Sometimes people like drugs or need drugs so much they can't do without them. They are dependent upon drugs. Only a few kinds of drugs, like narcotics, can cause physical dependence. But almost any drug, when it is misused, can make a person think he needs it all the time. By this time it is too late and the person is "hooked."

Tobacco, alcohol, and marijuana are three common drugs. These three are called the "gateway drugs." They are the first ones most people use and become dependent on.

Recalling Facts

1. A drug is a
   - ☐ a. chemical.
   - ☐ b. mineral.
   - ☐ c. vegetable.

2. The drug found in coffee and tea is called
   - ☐ a. alcohol.
   - ☐ b. caffeine.
   - ☐ c. marijuana.

3. People who take drugs only at parties are called
   - ☐ a. dependent users.
   - ☐ b. experimental users.
   - ☐ c. recreational users.

4. When people can't do without drugs, they are
   - ☐ a. dependent.
   - ☐ b. independent.
   - ☐ c. misused.

5. Tobacco, alcohol, and marijuana are called the
   - ☐ a. escape drugs.
   - ☐ b. gateway drugs.
   - ☐ c. service drugs.

Understanding the Passage

6. What is the main idea of this article?
   - ☐ a. Drug abuse is on the rise in America.
   - ☐ b. It helps to know something about drugs.
   - ☐ c. The use of marijuana should be made legal.

7. The writer makes this passage clear by using
   - ☐ a. facts.
   - ☐ b. numbers.
   - ☐ c. stories.

8. This passage hints that drug abuse can cause
   - ☐ a. hair loss.
   - ☐ b. physical pain.
   - ☐ c. sleeping sickness.

9. We can see that drugs
   - ☐ a. are made from herbs.
   - ☐ b. can be dangerous.
   - ☐ c. are easy to make.

10. Narcotics can cause
    - ☐ a. cold sores.
    - ☐ b. normal breathing.
    - ☐ c. physical dependence.

Many people have never seen a goat, but there are more than 400 million goats on earth. Goats are easier to keep than cows. They do not need as much space to live in, and they do not need large areas of grass for food. Goats like to eat trees and leaves. They are good at climbing rocky ledges. Often very poor farmland can support a goat.

There are many varieties of domestic goats. Farmers raise most of these goats for both milk and meat. But many people like them as pets, too. When you see a goat, look at its ears. If it has straight ears, it might be an Alpine. ●
Floppy ears belong to Nubians. And a LaMancha has no ears at all. Some goats are raised for their fancy wool. Angora and Cashmere goats have fine, silky fleeces. Look at the label on your coat or sweater. It might say "mohair" or "cashmere" on it. Then you know you have a goat to thank.

There are many things to learn about goat care. Goats are very clean animals. They like sunny, dry barns, so never keep a goat in a damp pen. It can catch a cold just like a person can. It is important to control your ●
goat's diet. Make sure it has plenty of green hay. It will also enjoy grain. And a goat always needs a bucket of fresh water. Strong fences are a must. Goats love to jump, and they can also crawl under a loose fence. You may discover your flowers eaten if she gets out!

Goats are very curious animals. They are also intelligent. Scientists say that a goat is as smart as a dog. It will come when called by name. It will also let you know who its favorite people are. ●

You can visit goat farms all over America, but you can see goats in other places, too. A fair is an excellent spot to see a lot of goats. Fairs often have special goat shows. Prizes go to the finest animals in each breed. The goats are judged on their looks and grooming. Often prizes are given for high milk production. These goat shows usually include both adult and kid goats. All kids are under one year old. The goat owners are very proud of their animals. They will be glad to talk to you about goats.

Recalling Facts

1. Scientists say that a goat is as smart as a
   - ☐ a. rabbit.
   - ☐ b. dog.
   - ☐ c. human.

2. A goat without any ears is called
   - ☐ a. a Nubian.
   - ☐ b. an Alpine.
   - ☑ c. a LaMancha.

3. Angora goats are primarily raised for their
   - ☐ a. wool.
   - ☐ b. milk.
   - ☐ c. meat.

4. As far as goat farming is concerned, strong fences are
   - ☐ a. important.
   - ☐ b. unimportant.
   - ☐ c. useless.

5. Goat shows judge animals on
   - ☐ a. weight.
   - ☐ b. intelligence.
   - ☐ c. looks.

Understanding the Passage

6. Cows need
   - ☐ a. rocky ledges to climb.
   - ☐ b. large areas of grass for food.
   - ☐ c. very little space.

7. Mohair is a kind of
   - ☐ a. label.
   - ☐ b. food.
   - ☑ c. wool.

8. How might a goat catch a cold?
   - ☐ a. drinking cold water
   - ☐ b. sleeping in a damp pen
   - ☐ c. going to a goat show

9. The article suggests that it is important to
   - ☐ a. let your goat run loose.
   - ☐ b. buy only cashmere sweaters.
   - ☑ c. make sure your goat has plenty of hay.

10. Goats and cows need
    - ☐ a. different care.
    - ☐ b. the same care.
    - ☐ c. little care.

3 minut

7/10

35 A Measure in Metrics

What do metric measures mean to you? They could mean a lot. Some time soon, the United States might adopt the metric system. Some countries have already made the switch. As the use of metric measures increases, you will see a change in your nearby food store. You will see metric units used for weight, volume, and length.

Many people say the change makes sense. Right now, the number of different units you meet in a day's shopping is confusing. Weights are shown in ounces and pounds. Liquids are measured in gallons, quarts, pints, and fluid ounces. Dry measures are shown in bushels, pecks, dry quarts, and pints. But all of that would be easier under the metric system. With metric units, weight is shown only in grams or kilograms. Volume is shown only in liters or kiloliters. Length is measured only in meters, centimeters, or millimeters. So metric seems much less confusing and easier to use when shopping.

Some of the most common measurements made in the home are those that take place in cooking and baking. The practice that is often followed in metric recipes is not so different from what we use now. Metric "cup and spoon" measures are only a bit larger than the cup and spoon measures we are used to. You can use either English or metric when you are cooking. It is only those few things now measured by weight (pounds and ounces) that will change a lot in the metric system. Changing a recipe to metric is easy. Just remember that a pound is about 450 grams and an ounce is about 28 grams.

Salespeople in hardware, paint, and fabric stores would feel the change to metric. A customer may want to buy lumber or paint or wallpaper. He or she may give the clerk the figures in English units. The clerk will have to know how to change them to metric. At least doing math in metric is not at all difficult. Again, it is easier to use than the English system.

The change to metric is coming. It should not scare you. It is an easy and simple system to use. For most people, the metric units they learn as customers will help them. Soon they will get used to the new system. Who knows? Maybe someday the English system will be completely forgotten.

Recalling Facts

1. Weights can be shown in ounces and
   - ☐ a. feet.
   - ☐ b. inches.
   - ☐ c. pounds.

2. Fluids are measured in
   - ☐ a. gallons.
   - ☐ b. pounds.
   - ☐ c. yards.

3. In metric labeling, weight will be shown only in grams or
   - ☐ a. kilograms.
   - ☐ b. kiloliters.
   - ☐ c. kilowatts.

4. Using the metric system, length will be measured in meters, centimeters, or
   - ☐ a. dekagrams.
   - ☐ b. kiloliters.
   - ☐ c. millimeters.

5. A pound is about
   - ☐ a. 100 grams.
   - ☐ b. 250 grams.
   - ☐ c. 450 grams.

Understanding the Passage

6. The metric system would be frequently used in
   - ☐ a. card shops.
   - ☐ b. grocery stores.
   - ☐ c. pet stores.

7. The metric system is
   - ☐ a. confusing to use.
   - ☐ b. easy to use.
   - ☐ c. hard to use.

8. This article hints that cooking and baking require a lot of
   - ☐ a. measuring.
   - ☐ b. preparing.
   - ☐ c. sampling.

9. We can see that salespeople will need to
   - ☐ a. know their customers.
   - ☐ b. learn the metric system.
   - ☐ c. travel a lot.

10. We can see that
   - ☐ a. cloth is often measured by the size of the bolt.
   - ☐ b. metric units are confusing and silly.
   - ☐ c. some people might be afraid to use the metric system.

36

Not Just for Graffiti

Paint sprayers are very useful for large surfaces. A spray gun is faster than a brush or a roller. Some paint may be wasted through overspraying. Even so, the time and effort saved more than make up for the extra paint. It takes a little time at first to learn how to spray. Once you have learned, it takes very little time at all to produce a thick and even coat of paint.

Spraying is a good way to cover surfaces that are rough and uneven. Things that are hard to paint with a brush or roller are quickly done with a sprayer. A spray gun can be used for any coat except the prime coat. The surface to be sprayed must be clean and free of dust. Paint that is sprayed will not stick if a film of dust is present.

Before you begin, ask your paint dealer to show you how the sprayer works. He will be able to give you some useful pointers. Adjust the gun so that the width of the spray is the same size as the surface to be covered. A narrow spray is best for small surfaces. A wide spray should be used for things like walls or tabletops.

Special care must be taken to prepare spray paint. Stir or strain the paint to remove any lumps. Be sure it is not too thick. Thick paint will clog the gun. But do not make the paint too thin, either. Thin paint will sag and run after it is sprayed. It is best to use the type and amount of thinner that is shown in the directions on the can.

Cover everything close to the work with drop cloths or newspapers. The "bounce-back" from the sprayer may spread several feet from the work surface. Be careful not to breathe in the paint dust. Use a mask to protect your lungs. When spraying, the tip of the spray gun may become clogged. Use a broom straw to clean it. Never use wire or a nail.

Hold the spray gun about eight inches from the surface to be painted. Start to spray while the gun is slightly beyond the surface. This assures an even flow when you reach the area to be coated. Move the sprayer parallel to the surface. Spray the corners and edges first. Then direct the stream evenly back and forth across the area.

Recalling Facts

1. Paint sprayers are best for painting
   - ☐ a. narrow trims.
   - ☐ b. large surfaces.
   - ☐ c. small areas.

2. Before you spray a surface, it must be free of
   - ☐ a. dust.
   - ☐ b. paint.
   - ☐ c. scratches.

3. How far away from the surface to be painted should you hold the spray gun?
   - ☐ a. two inches
   - ☐ b. four inches
   - ☐ c. eight inches

4. A narrow spray is best for
   - ☐ a. rough surfaces.
   - ☐ b. uneven surfaces.
   - ☐ c. small surfaces.

5. If the tip of the spray gun becomes clogged, you can clear it with a
   - ☐ a. broom straw.
   - ☐ b. thin wire.
   - ☐ c. thick nail.

Understanding the Passage

6. A paint sprayer
   - ☐ a. is hard to use.
   - ☐ b. makes painting easier.
   - ☐ c. uses very little paint.

7. It seems that paint sprayers
   - ☐ a. do not do a good job on rough surfaces.
   - ☐ b. can never be used to paint small surfaces.
   - ☐ c. sometimes use a lot of paint.

8. Spray paint will not stick to a
   - ☐ a. clean surface.
   - ☐ b. dirty surface.
   - ☐ c. rough surface.

9. We can see that lumpy paint
   - ☐ a. keeps the paint sprayer working well.
   - ☐ b. makes the paint sprayer work better.
   - ☐ c. will eventually harm a paint sprayer.

10. The article hints that paint sprayers
    - ☐ a. are expensive to buy.
    - ☐ b. give off a fine paint dust.
    - ☐ c. use extra-thick paint.

37

You Aren't Getting Very Sleepy

When you hear the word "hypnosis," what comes to mind? Do you think of stage magicians who make people do silly things? Or do you think of evil creatures who force people to do wrong? Do you think of sleep-walking? Do you think of a medical technique? The last thing on the list is most likely not the first thing you thought of. Yet many doctors now use hypnosis. And those that do don't like all the wrong ideas people have about it.

The word comes from ancient Greece. "Hynos" was the god of sleep. But it's a mistake to think a hypnotic trance is like sleep. The phrase "you are getting very sleepy" is wrong. It may be heard in films or magic acts. But it's not what a doctor would say. In fact, a trance is almost the opposite of sleep. The person is very relaxed. But the mind is alert. The person is very aware of what is going on.

Franz Mesmer was the first doctor to use hypnosis. He lived more than two centuries ago. He hypnotized many patients. But many people doubted his ideas. They called him a fraud. Almost one hundred years later, a French doctor tried hypnosis. He used it as an anesthetic. He didn't use painkillers. He put people into a trance before surgery. He did this hundreds of times. His patients found they could control pain this way.

Maybe the most famous doctor to use hypnosis was Sigmund Freud. He used it as a tool to treat hysteria. This started the use of trances in treating mental problems. It was common for doctors to put patients in trances for this reason. But lately, many new uses have come about. Many doctors now think you can't separate the mind from the body. So it makes sense to use a mental technique to treat physical problems.

Many times, patients don't listen to their doctors. Or they might start to disagree. They are not open to new ideas. A doctor might say "You should cut down on sweets." The person thinks "I can't." But when in a trance, people are more open. They will try to change. The way this works is called "suggestion." The doctor may say the same things as before. But the patient accepts it better. Through suggestion, people can control eating, smoking, pain, and more. It is a successful medical technique.

Recalling Facts

1. The word "hypnotism" derives from
   - ☐ a. a medical technique.
   - ☐ b. the Greek god of sleep.
   - ☐ c. a relaxed trance state.

2. The first doctor to use hypnosis was
   - ☐ a. Franz Mesmer.
   - ☐ b. Sigmund Freud.
   - ☐ c. a French surgeon.

3. In a trance state, the person
   - ☐ a. is almost asleep.
   - ☐ b. feels no pain.
   - ☐ c. is very alert.

4. The most common medical use of hypnosis has been in
   - ☐ a. psychiatry.
   - ☐ b. surgery.
   - ☐ c. Mesmerism.

5. Hypnosis has been used in medicine
   - ☐ a. only in the 20th century.
   - ☐ b. since the 19th century.
   - ☐ c. since the 18th century.

Understanding the Passage

6. Many people equate hypnosis and sleep because
   - ☐ a. Hypnos was the Greek god of sleep.
   - ☐ b. magicians say "you are getting very sleepy."
   - ☐ c. the body is very relaxed, so the person may look asleep.

7. In this article, "hysteria" is the term for
   - ☐ a. crying and screaming.
   - ☐ b. a specific mental illness.
   - ☐ c. irrational behavior.

8. Hypnosis is a medical technique in the sense that
   - ☐ a. it can be used instead of anesthesia before surgery.
   - ☐ b. it can only be safely used by doctors.
   - ☐ c. doctors can use it to treat a variety of health problems.

9. The technique of "suggestion" can be used to
   - ☐ a. make people do things against their will.
   - ☐ b. help people respond better to things that are good for them.
   - ☐ c. suggest new and unusual ideas.

10. Hypnosis can be used to treat mental and physical problems because
    - ☐ a. the mind and body are closely interrelated.
    - ☐ b. it lowers the heart rate.
    - ☐ c. psychiatrists shared their ideas with other doctors.

38 Spiders

A spider is a small, eight-legged animal. Spiders are best known for the silk they spin. They use this silk to catch insects. Even large animals cannot escape from the sticky silk. Many spiders make webs. They use these webs as traps. If you look at a web, you can see the pretty patterns made by the spider.

But some spiders do not make webs. One kind of spider jumps onto an insect. Another spider uses its silk like a fishing line. It swings the line until it catches a bug. Then it reels up the line to eat its catch.

Spiders look like many of the insects they eat. But they are not insects. Spiders belong to a group called arachnids. All these animals have eight legs. None of them have feelers. Mites and ticks belong in this family.

Spiders lay eggs. Some large spiders lay 2,000 eggs at a time. One small spider lays just one egg. Many spiders die after they lay their eggs. The babies must learn to take care of themselves.

A lot of people are afraid of spiders, but only a few spiders can hurt humans. In fact, spiders are very helpful. They get rid of many harmful pests.

A tarantula is a kind of spider. It is large and hairy. You can find tarantulas in many warm climates. People in the South often see them. Once people thought that a tarantula's bite could give you a terrible disease. The person bitten by the tarantula might jump into the air. He or she might make strange noises. But this story is not true. Tarantulas in our country are quiet. This spider cannot hurt you any more than a bee can.

Some spiders really are very dangerous. The black widow is one of these spiders. Its bite is extremely painful. The bite can make you sick for a long time. Only the female black widow can hurt you. She has a shiny black body. It is about the size of a pea. Her long legs are very thin. If you turn her over, you can see a red or yellow mark on her body. But don't try to turn this spider over!

You can find black widows in almost every state. She often makes her webs in dark corners. This spider will not attack you. She will only bite if you bother her.

Recalling Facts

1. A spider has
   - ☐ a. six legs.
   - ☐ b. eight legs.
   - ☐ c. no legs.

2. Spiders belong to a family called
   - ☐ a. arachnids.
   - ☐ b. insects.
   - ☐ c. mites.

3. You can find a tarantula in
   - ☐ a. warm climates.
   - ☐ b. Canada.
   - ☐ c. the ocean.

4. One spider that can hurt you is a
   - ☐ a. tarantula.
   - ☐ b. black widow.
   - ☐ c. fishing spider.

5. The black widow is about the size of a
   - ☐ a. radish.
   - ☐ b. tarantula.
   - ☐ c. pea.

Understanding the Passage

6. All insects have
   - ☐ a. eight legs.
   - ☐ b. silk.
   - ☐ c. feelers.

7. Every spider uses its silk for
   - ☐ a. making webs.
   - ☐ b. catching insects.
   - ☐ c. climbing trees.

8. A tarantula
   - ☐ a. can give you a disease.
   - ☐ b. makes strange noises.
   - ☐ c. is not harmful.

9. If you see a black widow, you should
   - ☐ a. leave her alone.
   - ☐ b. turn her over.
   - ☐ c. bring her home to study.

10. Baby spiders are
    - ☐ a. poisonous.
    - ☐ b. dependent on their mothers.
    - ☐ c. able to take care of themselves.

39 Opportunity Knocks

Our country has many opportunities for adults who want to improve their lives. There are public schools you can attend. In the schools, you can take things like English, arithmetic, and history. You can find classes in almost any subject you want to study. You may want to learn to type, sew, paint, or fix TV sets. You may want to learn more about the trade you are already in. You may want to learn a new trade. You may want to get a high school diploma. You may even want to go to college. All it takes is time and effort. ●

In many cities, there are adult classes in the public schools. You can attend many of these classes without having to pay money. In some schools you may have to pay a small fee. There are also many kinds of private schools for adults.

In addition to schools, many industries and unions conduct on-the-job training programs. In these programs you hear about new ideas and learn new skills. Many large companies will send a worker to school if he or she has ability.

Many job opportunities are offered to those who wish to work. It helps if you know more than one language. There are good jobs for interpreters ● and typists who know English and another language.

There are many good jobs in government. In most cases, you must be a citizen of this country, and you must take a civil service examination. These examinations are open to everyone, regardless of race, religion, or color.

For many civil service jobs you need a high school diploma. The person who does not have a high school diploma can get one. There are several ways. You can study high school subjects at home and then take special tests. If you pass the tests, then you get a diploma. Or you can go to night ● school. There are classes that prepare you to take special tests to earn a diploma.

You can attend a night school that grants a high school diploma if you complete certain courses. If you do this, you do not have to take the special tests.

Be as well trained as you can. Get as much training as you can. Opportunity knocks at every door. Be sure that when it knocks at your door you are ready.

Recalling Facts

1. Our country has many
   opportunities for those who
   want to improve their
   ☐ a. diets.
   ☐ b. lives.
   ☐ c. personalities.

2. On-the-job training is often
   given by
   ☐ a. industries.
   ☐ b. libraries.
   ☐ c. schools.

3. Many large companies will
   send a worker to school if he
   or she has
   ☐ a. ability.
   ☐ b. friends.
   ☐ c. money.

4. If you know more than one
   language, you can get a job as
   ☐ a. a farmer.
   ☐ b. an interpreter.
   ☐ c. a lawyer.

5. In order to get a government
   job, you must take a
   ☐ a. course.
   ☐ b. test.
   ☐ c. trip.

Understanding the Passage

6. You can improve yourself
   by getting
   ☐ a. an education.
   ☐ b. a good diet.
   ☐ c. a piece of land.

7. In many places, public schooling
   for adults is
   ☐ a. difficult.
   ☐ b. free.
   ☐ c. new.

8. What does this article suggest?
   ☐ a. Any citizen can apply for a
      government job.
   ☐ b. Civil service jobs are offered
      only to foreigners.
   ☐ c. Training programs are often
      poorly organized.

9. We can see that
   ☐ a. one can work on a high
      school diploma at home.
   ☐ b. typists who know English
      earn a good pay.
   ☐ c. well-trained people are often
      out of a job.

10. Night school lets you
    ☐ a. go to school during the day
       and work at night.
    ☐ b. spend all your time studying.
    ☐ c. work and go to school at the
       same time.

40 A Handy-Dandy Tool

The jig saw is a good tool to have. It has a long, thin blade. This blade can cut corners or curves on a flat surface. Most jig saws for home use cost under $50. The blades on the cheaper saws move in an up-and-down motion. On more expensive saws, the blade swings out from the work on the downstroke and into the work for cutting on the upstroke. This motion makes the saw cut faster.

There are several kinds of jig saws. A light-duty jig saw can cut through 1½ inches of soft wood. It can cut through one inch of hard wood. Some jig saws can also handle soft metals that are one-eighth of an inch thick. These saws will stall or overheat if used to cut greater thicknesses. On the other hand, heavy-duty models can cut wood up to two inches and can be used on hard metals.

If you need to cut only simple shapes in wood or soft metals, a one-speed jig saw will do the job. For cutting harder metals, plastic, or fancy shapes, a two-speed model will help to protect the blade and give the user better control. But be careful!

Power tools, like jig saws, are handy tools, but they must be used properly. High-speed blades can cut and tear hands and feet as well as wood and metal. Electric current can burn and give shocks. Heat and sparks from tools can cause fires.

Before you begin using a tool, learn how it works and learn how to care for it. Read the manual that comes with it, and keep it nearby. Make sure the tool is the right one for the kind of work you are doing.

Keep the tool and cords away from heat, oil, and sharp edges that can hurt wires. Don't carry a tool by the cord. Don't jerk the cord to remove the plug from a wall outlet. You may break the cord if you do this. Never use a power tool near liquids that burn easily. Fumes from such liquids mix with air and can burst into flame from a spark that comes from the motor. When a tool overheats, it may start a fire inside the tool. When this happens, turn it off until it cools. Keep in mind that jig saws and other power tools make work easier but can also be dangerous.

Recalling Facts

1. The blade on a jig saw is
   - ☐ a. long and thin.
   - ☐ b. short and thin.
   - ☐ c. wide and short.

2. A jig saw cuts corners and curves on
   - ☐ a. a flat surface.
   - ☐ b. an oily surface.
   - ☐ c. a wet surface.

3. A light-duty jig saw can cut through 1½ inches of
   - ☐ a. hard wood.
   - ☐ b. sheet metal.
   - ☐ c. soft wood.

4. A two-speed jig saw is used to cut
   - ☐ a. hard metals.
   - ☐ b. soft metals.
   - ☐ c. glass.

5. You should always keep tool cords away from
   - ☐ a. heat.
   - ☐ b. metal.
   - ☐ c. wood.

Understanding the Passage

6. This article is mostly about
   - ☐ a. a power tool.
   - ☐ b. heavy-duty metals.
   - ☐ c. home repairs.

7. Expensive jig saws
   - ☐ a. cut faster than cheaper jig saws.
   - ☐ b. have many coats of paint on them.
   - ☐ c. work just as well as cheap jig saws.

8. If you use a light-duty jig saw on a thick metal, the saw will probably
   - ☐ a. move faster.
   - ☐ b. overheat.
   - ☐ c. sputter.

9. If not handled properly, the jig saw can
   - ☐ a. cause illness.
   - ☐ b. start fires.
   - ☐ c. stop mildew.

10. Jig saws are handy tools, but they can also be
    - ☐ a. beautiful.
    - ☐ b. dangerous.
    - ☐ c. heavy.

41 The Crunch is Coming

In the late 1970s, the United States felt the effects of an energy shortage. We felt it in higher gas prices. Many people had to wait in long lines at gas stations. Natural gas, electricity, and home heating oil prices all went up, too. Plants and businesses were forced to shut down. People were out of work. During the winter months, some people were without fuel to heat their homes. The problems were relieved for a time. But the energy crunch is not gone for good.

This is a big problem that affects all of us. And the solutions do not come ● easily. Oil and gas are not like trees. Trees can be replanted. But once oil and gas have been taken from the earth, they are gone forever. Of course, there will always be some oil and gas in the earth. But not all of this can be removed cheaply. In the U.S. most of the easy-to-reach oil and gas has been found. The supply that is left will cost much more to take from the ground.

Using less energy can help. If we all try to save on gas and oil, we can keep the energy problem under control. But even this will not keep us from ● running out. It will just keep us from running out sooner.

There are several other sources of energy we can turn to. Some can be used right away. Others need time. One source of energy we can use right now is coal. Coal is the largest fuel source in the U.S. In fact, this country has about one-third of the world's known supply of coal. Also, coal can be turned into gas and oil. But there are problems with coal. Burning coal can pollute the air. Coal mining is dangerous. Coal can be costly to ship. Plus, ● it can take up to seven years to open a new mine.

The sun is another source of energy. The sun is clean and does not need to be mined or drilled. But we have just begun to learn how to use the sun's energy. Because of this, it is expensive. For years to come, probably less than one-half of one percent of our energy needs will come from solar power. Sunshine is free. But solar energy has a long way to go before it can be used widely.

Recalling Facts

1. Plants have been forced
   to close down because of
   a lack of
   □ a. gas.
   □ b. machinery.
   □ c. workers.

2. In the past few winters, many
   people have run out of
   □ a. clothes.
   □ b. food.
   □ c. fuel.

3. Oil and gas are not like trees
   because oil and gas cannot be
   □ a. removed.
   □ b. replaced.
   □ c. reused.

4. One source of energy we can
   use right now is
   □ a. coal.
   □ b. gold.
   □ c. the sun.

5. Air can be polluted by
   □ a. burning coal.
   □ b. drilling oil wells.
   □ c. using solar energy.

Understanding the Passage

6. What is this article mostly about?
   □ a. energy
   □ b. mining
   □ c. pollution

7. We can see from this article that
   □ a. fuel is becoming scarce.
   □ b. oil wells are dangerous.
   □ c. solar energy is harmful.

8. The United States is rich in
   □ a. coal.
   □ b. gas.
   □ c. oil.

9. We have not yet learned
   how to use
   □ a. electricity.
   □ b. natural gas.
   □ c. solar power.

10. This article hints that solar
    energy will *not*
    □ a. damage buildings.
    □ b. cause illness.
    □ c. pollute the air.

42 You Get What You Pay For

We know that we have to pay for what we get. If we buy food, we have to pay for it. If a doctor treats us, we know there will be a bill to pay. These are private bills. But there are also public bills that must be paid. Public bills are paid for by the government. In turn we get needed services. We all use these services without thinking how we get them. But such services cost money. We pay for these services through taxes.

What would happen if everyone in a city stopped paying taxes? The water supply would stop. Water might even become unclean and impure. The streets might not be cleaned. There would be no police force to protect people and property. Schools would be closed. People would become sick and disease might spread. We would not want to live in such a city. We all want pure water and food, clean streets, and good schools. We want police to protect us from crime.

These services are expensive. The bills get larger each year. We spend public money today for services that we did not have fifty years ago. For instance, we now use public money to help stop accidents in mines and shops and to help farmers.

The chief duty of every government is to protect persons and property. More than three-fourths of the money spent by our government is used for this purpose. The next largest amount of public money goes to teach and train our citizens. Billions of dollars each year are spent on schools and libraries. Public money is used to pay the teachers and other public officials. Also, a large amount of public funds is spent on roads.

The greatest part of the needed funds is raised by taxes. A tax is money that we all must pay to support the government. The law orders us to pay taxes. We have no choice in the matter. Almost everyone pays some tax in one form or another.

Years ago, the government made money from the sale of public lands. But most of the best public lands have now been sold. The money raised was used to help pay the costs of government. There are still some public lands that contain oil, coal, gas, and other natural products. They could be sold. But we want to save them for future years. So, we all must pay our share for the services that make our lives comfortable.

Recalling Facts

1. A doctor's bill is a
   - ☐ a. popular bill.
   - ☐ b. private bill.
   - ☐ c. public bill.

2. Government services are
   paid for by
   - ☐ a. interest.
   - ☐ b. loans.
   - ☐ c. taxes.

3. Public money is used to stop
   accidents in
   - ☐ a. homes.
   - ☐ b. mines.
   - ☐ c. stores.

4. The chief duty of every
   government is to protect
   persons and
   - ☐ a. automobiles.
   - ☐ b. property.
   - ☐ c. livestock.

5. Years ago, the government
   raised money by selling
   - ☐ a. gas.
   - ☐ b. guns.
   - ☐ c. land.

Understanding the Passage

6. Which of these would be a good
   title for this article?
   - ☐ a. Government Services
     and Taxes
   - ☐ b. Protection from Crime
   - ☐ c. Schools and Libraries Are
     Public

7. Taxes pay for
   - ☐ a. doctor's bills.
   - ☐ b. private bills.
   - ☐ c. public bills.

8. Most of the money spent by the
   government is spent to
   - ☐ a. clean the water supply.
   - ☐ b. protect people and property.
   - ☐ c. teach and train people.

9. This article suggests that
   - ☐ a. even the rich pay taxes.
   - ☐ b. government land is cheap.
   - ☐ c. people do not like the police.

10. What could happen if people did
    not pay taxes?
    - ☐ a. Cities would become dirty.
    - ☐ b. The police would be
      better trained.
    - ☐ c. Schools would hire
      more teachers.

43 Pile It On

Most people want to know just one thing when they use a vacuum cleaner. Does it pick up dirt? How well a vacuum works depends mostly on how well you use it.

Before you vacuum, you should pick up all small, hard, or sharp objects. These include things like clips or pins which might harm the blades or the hose or put a hole in the dust bag. Check the dust bag. Empty it or put on a new one if it is full. A clean bag will help the cleaner do a better job and will protect the motor.

Remove any hairs or threads from the brushes. If long threads are wound around the brush, cut them in several places. Short pieces of thread can be pulled out easily.

An upright vacuum cleaner has controls that have to be set to the height of the pile of the rug. The nozzle should ride just above the pile. Too low a setting will make the cleaner hard to push. It will cause the rug to wear out faster, too. Too high a setting will not give the rug a deep cleaning. Check the brushes for wear. If they are worn, adjust them or replace them. Check the belt that drives the brushes. When it becomes stretched or starts to crack or wear thin, it will not work properly.

When you use the vacuum, listen to the sound it makes. If there is a change in the sound, switch the motor off. There may be a problem with the air flow. You could burn out the motor if you keep it running. Turn the vacuum off if it gets hot or if there is a drop in the suction. See if the bag needs changing or needs to be emptied. The cleaner works best when the dust bag is clean. Don't let the bag get too full. When picking up fine dust, such as flour or soot, the bag clogs more quickly. You will have to change the bag more often. Check to see if any of the air passages are clogged. If the vacuum heats up, see if the brush is clogged with lint or hair. Check to be sure the belt has not come off the pulley.

When you are finished, store the vacuum in a dry place. Keep the hose on a shelf or hang it over two hooks spaced well apart.

Recalling Facts

1. Before you vacuum, you should pick up all
   - ☐ a. fine dust.
   - ☐ b. loose hairs.
   - ☐ c. sharp objects.

2. Pins might put a hole in the vacuum's
   - ☐ a. cord.
   - ☐ b. hose.
   - ☐ c. motor.

3. A clean dust bag protects the vacuum's
   - ☐ a. brushes.
   - ☐ b. cord.
   - ☐ c. motor.

4. If a vacuum gets very hot, you should
   - ☐ a. fill the dust bag.
   - ☐ b. put water on it.
   - ☐ c. turn it off.

5. The dust bag of a vacuum clogs more quickly when it picks up
   - ☐ a. crumbs.
   - ☐ b. hair.
   - ☐ c. soot.

Understanding the Passage

6. What is this article mostly about?
   - ☐ a. caring for your vacuum cleaner
   - ☐ b. different kinds of vacuum cleaners
   - ☐ c. the history of vacuum cleaners

7. A vacuum cleaner will not work well if the
   - ☐ a. dust bag is full.
   - ☐ b. hose is clean.
   - ☐ c. motor is oiled.

8. The pile of a rug has to do with the rug's
   - ☐ a. backing.
   - ☐ b. size.
   - ☐ c. thickness.

9. A cracked vacuum belt must be
   - ☐ a. dried.
   - ☐ b. oiled.
   - ☐ c. replaced.

10. A vacuum cleaner may overheat if there is a problem with the
    - ☐ a. air flow.
    - ☐ b. current.
    - ☐ c. pile setting.

44   A Pest Problem

Pesticides are chemicals that kill. They can slow or stop the growth of pests. Pests can be insects, fish, rats, mice, fungi, weeds, and other harmful animals or plants. Pests are bad because they spoil food. They ruin clothes, household goods, and buildings. They spread disease. They can injure and kill people. Pests can also harm helpful animals and plants.

Helpful animals and plants are those that people like and make use of. Or they are ones that are vital to a healthy world. These might be living things that give us food, such as crops and cattle. They also could be house plants, or cats and dogs kept as pets. In this group are the animals and plants found in nature that people like. And some forms of life are needed to keep a smooth and even balance. So, to protect plants and animals from harm, we use pesticides.

Pesticides are helpful. But they can be harmful, too. Pesticides can be misused. They can be used without following the right directions. When this happens, they do a great deal of harm to the animals and plants that we want to keep. Pesticides can poison. The deadly effects of these poisons can last a long time. The remains of some pesticides last for many years. They harm and kill long after they were first used.

The message is clear. Pesticides are useful. They take care of us and our useful plants and animals. But if not used in the right way, pesticides can cause a lot of harm. You can never be too careful when using pesticides.

Guard yourself and others from pesticides. It is not safe for children to use them. In some cases, it is against the law. Pest control is a job for grown-ups. Teach your child well. Children should be able to know a pesticide by the label on the package. They should be taught not to use empty pesticide jars or cans. Spilled pesticide on the outside of the jar can be unsafe. It can poison someone. Keep poisons out of reach of small children.

Sometimes people are poisoned by a pesticide. If this happens, directions on the label will tell you what to do. Follow them carefully.

Ways to control pests without using pesticides need to be found and tested. Perhaps in the future we will learn to control pests in a better way.

Recalling Facts

1. Pesticides are
   - ☐ a. chemicals.
   - ☐ b. minerals.
   - ☐ c. vitamins.

2. Pests spoil
   - ☐ a. food.
   - ☐ b. paint.
   - ☐ c. oil.

3. Which of the following are pests?
   - ☐ a. cattle
   - ☐ b. dogs
   - ☐ c. fungi

4. Pesticides should never be used by
   - ☐ a. adults.
   - ☐ b. children.
   - ☐ c. people.

5. If someone is poisoned by a pesticide, you should follow the directions on the
   - ☐ a. handle.
   - ☐ b. label.
   - ☐ c. lid.

Understanding the Passage

6. What is the main idea of this article?
   - ☐ a. Harmful pests do much damage to clothing.
   - ☐ b. Pesticides can be helpful as well as harmful.
   - ☐ c. Useful animals often carry many diseases.

7. Some people like to decorate their houses with
   - ☐ a. pests.
   - ☐ b. plants.
   - ☐ c. poison.

8. This article hints that pesticides are
   - ☐ a. easy to use.
   - ☐ b. expensive to buy.
   - ☐ c. harmful to children.

9. Often pesticides are dangerous because they
   - ☐ a. are not used properly.
   - ☐ b. are stored in the garage.
   - ☐ c. explode easily.

10. New ways to control pests
    - ☐ a. need to be tested.
    - ☐ b. are easily found.
    - ☐ c. are not needed.

45   Cozy Covers

Each of us spends about one third of our life in bed. Over 45 million homes now use electric blankets for sleeping at night. The cost of using an electric blanket is small. On a middle setting the cost is no more than half a cent for all night. This is much less than the cost of keeping the heat high in the bedroom.

Few people know that an electric blanket does not heat you up at night. The truth is that the blanket stops the loss of body heat. The blanket provides a warm layer of air which keeps the heat in. The body itself does most of the work.

However, life was not always so cozy beneath the covers. People once shivered as they slept. To keep warm, early man used animal hides and campfires. Later on, fireplaces and wool blankets were used. Around 1600, another improvement came on the scene. This aid was the warming pan. Hot coals were put into a flat pan. Then, the pan was moved around under the sheets to warm the bed. Still later, someone invented the feather-filled comforter. This new kind of blanket used the body's heat to warm the bed.

But the first real breakthrough came when boilers were brought into the home in the 19th century. Radiators were used to heat each room. It was a welcome improvement. This meant that the heat for the whole home could be controlled.

Then late in the 1800s, electric blankets came on the scene. They arrived just after the boilers. But these early blankets were not meant to give comfort to the user. Rather, they were for medical use. At that time, doctors felt that the more the cure hurt, the better for the patient. Electric blankets were used to make patients sweat. Sweating was thought to drive out germs.

Hospitals were some of the first to use the new blankets. Sometimes patients had to sleep outside on porches. The blankets were used to protect them from cold and snow. There is no record of the number of people who lived through this. But the cure was probably worse than the illness.

Electric blankets now come in all sizes. They are light, warm, and clean. Stores sell a lot of them. It seems we've come a long way since furs and skins. So let's hear it for the things that now make sleep better.

*Reading Time*_____ *Comprehension Score*_____ *Words per Minute*_____   103

Recalling Facts

1. How many American homes now use electric blankets?
   - ☐ a. about 10 million
   - ☐ b. around 30 million
   - ☐ c. over 45 million

2. What is the nightly cost of using an electric blanket?
   - ☐ a. half a cent
   - ☐ b. a nickel
   - ☐ c. twelve cents

3. An electric blanket keeps you warm by preventing a loss of body
   - ☐ a. fat.
   - ☐ b. fluid.
   - ☐ c. heat.

4. The warming pan came into use around
   - ☐ a. 1400.
   - ☐ b. 1500.
   - ☐ c. 1600.

5. Radiators were invented in the
   - ☐ a. 15th century.
   - ☐ b. 19th century.
   - ☐ c. 20th century.

Understanding the Passage

6. This article hints that electric blankets
   - ☐ a. are dangerous.
   - ☐ b. save energy.
   - ☐ c. stop disease.

7. Today more people are using electric blankets because of
   - ☐ a. their bright colors.
   - ☐ b. the oil shortage.
   - ☐ c. their low price.

8. We can see that early man had trouble keeping
   - ☐ a. clean.
   - ☐ b. healthy.
   - ☐ c. warm.

9. The feather-filled comforter was a better investment than
   - ☐ a. electric blankets.
   - ☐ b. radiators.
   - ☐ c. warming pans.

10. Electric blankets were once used to
    - ☐ a. decorate floors.
    - ☐ b. cure sick people.
    - ☐ c. cover tables.

46   Healthy, Happy Trees

Healthy trees are important to us all. Trees provide shade, beauty, and homes for wildlife. Trees give us products like paper and wood. Trees can give us all this only if they are healthy. They must be well cared for to remain healthy.

Your tree's trouble may be you. People spend much time and money to plant and maintain trees. Trees improve the looks of homes, parks, businesses, and public buildings. Yet, people who love trees the most may be the ones who cause them injury. Of course, they do not do this on purpose. They are most likely not aware of the kinds of things that injure trees. There are many people-caused tree injuries. You should become aware of them and avoid them. Learn the things that can help to keep your trees healthy.

Healthy trees are beautiful. They make our world a pleasant place to live in. Unhealthy trees are not as beautiful. They make the world less pleasant. Healthy trees help to cool and clean the air. They can even deaden sound. Unhealthy trees cannot help or protect the environment. Trees, like people, are disturbed by changes around them. Construction of buildings is a major cause of tree injury.

Signs of tree disease may not be seen right away. Sometimes it takes many years for an injured tree to die. Trees are often injured by changes in ground level. Roots can be damaged when heavy building equipment passes over them. Root injury, not trunk injury, during construction is most likely to kill trees.

When homes are built, concrete, bricks, or too much soil is put around trees. This can change the amount of water and air that the roots get. Trees with roots covered in this way cannot "breathe." They die within three to five years. Putting a small well around the trunk of a young tree may help. A young tree planted in a large well can adapt to living in a well. When young trees are to be planted within large paved areas, such as parking lots, they should be planted in large wells. Trees should not be planted until all construction has been completed.

You can prevent damage to older trees near construction sites by putting fences around them. You can tell workers to be extra careful when working close to trees. Remember, careless building and road construction kill trees.

Recalling Facts

1. Trees give us products like
   - ☐ a. cotton.
   - ☑ b. paper.
   - ☐ c. plastic.

2. Healthy trees help to keep the air
   - ☑ a. clean.
   - ☐ b. dusty.
   - ☐ c. stale.

3. Trees are often injured by changes in the
   - ☐ a. ground level.
   - ☑ b. seasons.
   - ☐ c. water table.

4. If tree roots are covered by concrete or bricks, the tree cannot
   - ☑ a. breathe.
   - ☐ b. blossom.
   - ☐ c. bud.

5. Careless building and road construction can
   - ☐ a. help trees.
   - ☑ b. kill trees.
   - ☐ c. improve trees.

Understanding the Passage

6. Choose the best title for this article.
   - ☑ a. Don't Injure That Tree
   - ☐ b. Firewood is Best
   - ☐ c. Forest Fires Hurt

7. This article hints that people often
   - ☑ a. harm trees without knowing it.
   - ☐ b. plant trees at the wrong time.
   - ☐ c. start many forest fires.

8. We can see that during the summer, healthy trees help to keep us
   - ☐ a. busy.
   - ☐ b. cool.
   - ☐ c. warm.

9. Unhealthy trees may look
   - ☐ a. beautiful.
   - ☐ b. spotless.
   - ☐ c. ugly.

10. Construction can harm a tree because it
    - ☑ a. disturbs the ground around a tree.
    - ☐ b. puts a lot of extra heat into the ground.
    - ☐ c. sends harmful dust into the air.

Clean Carpets Live Longer

Your new rug deserves and needs good care. To do this, you should follow a home cleaning program. A light cleaning once a day with a carpet sweeper or vacuum cleaner is a good idea. This stops dirt from working down between the pile yarns. Once in the rug, dirt can cut fibers or reach the backing. Of course, often-used areas will need more thorough cleaning. Once a week, all rugs should get a good cleaning. Five to seven strokes of a vacuum cleaner over each area is best. Thick pile carpet may need even more.

At times you may wish to use a chemical cleaner. Chemical cleaners help remove grit and greasy soil that dull carpet colors. If you decide to do this, be sure you buy cleaners that are made for rugs. You should not use soap, ammonia, or bleach. And don't use household cleaners that are made for hard surfaces. These may make colors run. They can also damage the yarn. There are three types of cleaners that you can use at home. They are shampoo, foam spray, and powder. Shampoo can be put on with a hand machine. Or you can rent power equipment. Don't use too much shampoo. Don't shampoo too often.

Be sure the carpet has a chance to dry. If the backing does not dry thoroughly, it may mildew. In mild weather, open the windows.

You may choose to use foam instead of shampoo. Do one area at a time. Spray the foam on the carpet in a thin layer. Then rub it in right away with a sponge. After it has dried, you can remove the dirt by vacuuming. If you use a powder cleaner, vacuum the carpet first. Next, sprinkle on the powder. Brush it into the pile, let it dry, and vacuum. Powders soak up greasy soil. They won't cause colors to fade or run, and they won't cause backing to mildew.

In spite of good home care, carpets may need occasional expert cleaning. Unless you have wall-to-wall carpet, you can send your rugs to a rug cleaning plant. The backing and the pile can both be cleaned this way. Wall-to-wall carpet must be cleaned in the home. Hire someone who has the equipment to do the job right. A skilled person will know how to remove grease and dirt and bring out the beauty of your carpet.

Recalling Facts

1. You should clean your carpet daily with a
   - ☐ a. chemical shampoo.
   - ☐ b. hand brush.
   - ☐ c. vacuum cleaner.

2. Greasy soil
   - ☐ a. breaks carpet fibers.
   - ☐ b. dulls carpet colors.
   - ☐ c. softens carpet yarn.

3. Which of the following should be used to clean a carpet?
   - ☐ a. ammonia
   - ☐ b. hand soap
   - ☐ c. rug shampoo

4. If the backing of a carpet does not dry thoroughly, it may
   - ☐ a. discolor.
   - ☐ b. mildew.
   - ☐ c. shrink.

5. Foam shampoo should be rubbed into the carpet with a
   - ☐ a. brush.
   - ☐ b. rag.
   - ☐ c. sponge.

Understanding the Passage

6. This article suggests that
   - ☐ a. dirt can harm a carpet.
   - ☐ b. good carpets are expensive.
   - ☐ c. carpets must always be professionally cleaned.

7. Some household cleaners can
   - ☐ a. damage a carpet.
   - ☐ b. not keep a carpet clean.
   - ☐ c. soil a carpet.

8. Opening a window helps to
   - ☐ a. dry a wet carpet.
   - ☐ b. fade carpet colors.
   - ☐ c. keep the carpet wet.

9. Powder rug shampoos are good because they
   - ☐ a. are cheap and easy to use.
   - ☐ b. soak into the carpet and backing.
   - ☐ c. won't fade a carpet's colors.

10. Wall-to-wall carpet must be cleaned in the home because it is
    - ☐ a. attached to the floor.
    - ☐ b. likely to be lost.
    - ☐ c. too dirty to move.

At one time or another we have all stopped to think about the weather. Some days the weather is good. Some days the weather is bad. Still, there are days when the weather seems to change from hour to hour. A day that starts out fine might not stay that way. Sometimes a day that seems bad turns out better than you thought it would. There are ways of understanding the weather. One way is to study the clouds.

No two clouds are ever alike. But it is still possible to group clouds and to give them names. We can recognize the different kinds of clouds and watch them for signs of changing weather.

As a rule, the higher the clouds, the better the weather. And the lower the clouds, the worse the weather is likely to be. To predict the weather, there are three things about clouds you should look for: movement, color, and change.

Clouds can tell you if a storm is on the way. For example, small, feathery cirrus clouds can become thick and move lower. This means rain is on the way. If the thick, fluffy cumulus clouds get bigger early in the day, then you know it will rain. If there's a sudden, cool breeze and a dark thunder cloud appears, then a storm is about to break out.

Clouds are not only signs of storms and rain. They may also be signs of good weather. The cirrus cloud may stay high in the sky and move very slowly. This means fine weather. Fair-weather cumulus clouds are another sign of good weather. These are the clouds we often see on warm summer days.

Colors in the sky tell us about the weather, too. A golden ring around the moon warns us that a storm is on the way. A watery, yellow sunset is a sign that rain may be near.

The rainbow has a message, too. The colors of the rainbow come from sun rays shining through falling rain. If you see the sun in the east and a rainbow in the west, the rain may be coming your way. If the sun is in the west and the rainbow is in the east, the rain will be moving away from you.

Clouds and the colors in the sky show signs of changing weather. Knowing a little about them both can help you become weather wise.

Recalling Facts

1. One way to understand the weather is to study the
   - ☐ a. clouds.
   - ☐ b. temperature.
   - ☐ c. wind.

2. High clouds mean
   - ☐ a. nice weather.
   - ☐ b. rainy weather.
   - ☐ c. snowy weather.

3. A small cirrus cloud that is moving lower is a sign of
   - ☐ a. rain.
   - ☐ b. snow.
   - ☐ c. wind.

4. What kind of cloud usually appears on a warm summer day?
   - ☐ a. cirrus
   - ☐ b. cumulus
   - ☐ c. stratus

5. A rainbow results when the sun shines through falling
   - ☐ a. hail.
   - ☐ b. rain.
   - ☐ c. snow.

Understanding the Passage

6. If you study the clouds in the sky, then you should be able to
   - ☐ a. exercise regularly.
   - ☐ b. predict the weather.
   - ☐ c. stop a drought.

7. This article hints that
   - ☐ a. even though no two clouds are alike, they can be named.
   - ☐ b. high clouds often bring us stormy and windy weather.
   - ☐ c. weathermen know very little about weather patterns.

8. Low hanging clouds signal
   - ☐ a. bad weather.
   - ☐ b. good weather.
   - ☐ c. unchanging weather.

9. When we see a golden ring around the moon, we can expect
   - ☐ a. calm weather.
   - ☐ b. sunny weather.
   - ☐ c. stormy weather.

10. Which of these would be a good title for this article?
    - ☐ a. History of Weather Forecasting
    - ☐ b. New England Weather
    - ☐ c. Good Weather and Bad

Many people will say that the worst thing about moving is . . . moving! It's difficult to search for a new job or school, or to buy a new home. It's really hard to make new friends. But packing and moving seems the hardest thing of all.

You can hire people to do your packing. But most people are reluctant to do this. For one thing, it's very expensive. For another thing, how can you find things you need in the new location if someone else put them in the boxes? The advantage of having professionals pack for you is that they have all the right materials. They never run out of boxes or tissue ●
paper. They even have special boxes made just for mirrors, dishes, and other breakables.

If you pack yourself, there are lots of tips to follow. Don't take everything. Moving time is a good time to sort out junk. Have a yard sale, or give things away. If you give things to charity, you may get a tax deduction. This is a good time to get organized. Sort everything out. Don't just throw things together in a jumble. Pack similar things together, or things that go in the ●
same area. And be sure to label the boxes. There are two ways to do this. The easiest is to write a short description of the contents and where it's going right on the box. For example, "Clothes—master bedroom." A more precise way to label is to write a number on each box. On a sheet of paper, list all the numbers. Then write down the contents of each box. This is a lot of work. But it's a great help if you use a professional mover and any boxes are lost.

Even if they pack their own things, most people hire a professional ●
mover. It's just too hard to drive a big truck. And carrying so many boxes is too tiring.

To choose a mover, check the phone book for three or four names. Then call the Better Business Bureau to see if there are complaints logged against these movers. Ask friends and neighbors for their input, too. And talk to the movers. Don't just ask about price. Ask about how they pack valuables. Ask about insurance coverage. Go over all the details of the contract.

If you take care in planning, your move will go more smoothly.

---

*Reading Time*_____ *Comprehension Score*_____ *Words per Minute*_____

Recalling Facts

1. An advantage to having your movers pack for you is that
   - ☐ a. they never lose things.
   - ☐ b. they have all the right materials.
   - ☐ c. it saves you time.

2. You may get a tax deduction by
   - ☐ a. hiring a non-profit moving company.
   - ☐ b. having a yard sale.
   - ☐ c. donating items to charity.

3. Pack things together that
   - ☐ a. belong in the same place.
   - ☐ b. aren't too heavy.
   - ☐ c. are breakable.

4. The first place to look for names of movers is
   - ☐ a. newspaper ads.
   - ☐ b. the Better Business Bureau.
   - ☐ c. the phone book.

5. Your move will go more smoothly if you
   - ☐ a. hire a professional.
   - ☐ b. plan carefully.
   - ☐ c. get help from friends and neighbors.

Understanding the Passage

6. Why should similar things be packed together?
   - ☐ a. They'll fit into the same box more easily.
   - ☐ b. It makes unpacking more convenient.
   - ☐ c. The movers tell you to.

7. The best reason to label the boxes themselves is because
   - ☐ a. the movers will be more careful if they know what's inside.
   - ☐ b. the boxes won't get lost as easily.
   - ☐ c. it's much easier to find what you need and to unpack later.

8. The best reason to keep a separate list of the boxes is because
   - ☐ a. it's an organized way to know everything you own.
   - ☐ b. if things are lost, you know what's missing.
   - ☐ c. you can sort out the boxes in the new location.

9. If the Better Business Bureau has no record of complaints about the moving companies you are looking at, you
   - ☐ a. can be guaranteed of a safe move.
   - ☐ b. should still investigate further.
   - ☐ c. should tell the movers they have a good reputation.

10. The most important thing to consider when hiring a mover is who
    - ☐ a. can do the job for the least money.
    - ☐ b. can deliver your belongings soonest.
    - ☐ c. will offer fair terms and take care of your belongings.

50 "I Scream, You Scream . . ."

Most people know that kids' rhyme. It ends ". . . we all scream for ice cream." Kids have shouted those words for more than 50 years. Ice cream has been, and still is, the favorite dessert of children.

It is almost as much fun to make ice cream as to eat it. And it's almost as easy, too. Even young children can help make this frozen treat.

There are three basic ingredients in homemade ice cream. Of course, cream is the main ingredient. Then sugar or some other sweetener is added. Third is flavoring. This can be almost anything. The most common are vanilla extract and cocoa or chocolate syrup. But lots of cooks have tried instant coffee or fresh fruit. Even crushed candies or peanut butter can be put in ice cream.

Hundreds of other goodies have been used in ice cream.

To make a healthier dessert, don't even use cream. Ice milk is also delicious. Or try frozen yogurt. Or make your own sherbet using milk and fruit juice. Europeans make sorbet. This is a frozen juice treat. It has no dairy products.

Whether you make real ice cream or a low-fat frozen dessert, the technique is pretty much the same. The easiest way to make ice cream is to use a freezer made just for this purpose. The ice cream freezer does two basic things. It chills the ingredients enough to make them freeze solid. And it also stirs the mix so it is smooth and creamy.

You can make ice cream without an ice-cream freezer. You can just put the mix in your freezer. This will get it cold enough to be solid. But if you don't stir it, it won't be smooth. It would be like making flavored ice. It might taste good, but it would be too hard.

Still, you can make ice cream without a special machine. Just take the cream mixture out of the freezer before it gets really hard. Stir it well to break up the ice crystals. Do this three or four times. When you let it freeze hard, it will be smooth.

It's even easier to make ice cream with a machine. Just put the flavored cream mixture into the cannister, then surround the cannister with ice and salt. The salt hastens the chilling. Turn the machine on. It automatically stirs and freezes. You'll have ice cream in 20 minutes.

*Reading Time*_____ *Comprehension Score*_____ *Words per Minute*_____ 113

Recalling Facts

1. The main ingredients in ice cream are cream,
   - ☐ a. sugar, and chocolate.
   - ☐ b. sweetener, and vanilla.
   - ☐ c. sweetener, and flavoring.

2. Sorbet is
   - ☐ a. the European word for sherbet.
   - ☐ b. sweetened ice milk.
   - ☐ c. frozen fruit juice dessert.

3. The difference between ice cream and ice milk is
   - ☐ a. you use milk in place of the cream.
   - ☐ b. ice milk uses more sugar.
   - ☐ c. there are more flavors of ice milk available.

4. The most popular ice cream flavors are
   - ☐ a. fruit and sherbet.
   - ☐ b. coffee and chocolate.
   - ☐ c. vanilla and chocolate.

5. Salt is put on the ice to
   - ☐ a. add extra flavor.
   - ☐ b. speed up the freezing.
   - ☐ c. help preserve the finished product.

Understanding the Passage

6. A major reason for buying an ice cream machine is that they
   - ☐ a. are so inexpensive.
   - ☐ b. can make a variety of flavors.
   - ☐ c. work quickly.

7. Ice milk and sherbet are considered healthier than ice cream because they
   - ☐ a. have less fat and cholesterol.
   - ☐ b. use fresh fruits.
   - ☐ c. use less sugar.

8. The reason stirring produces smoother ice cream is
   - ☐ a. all the ingredients are distributed evenly.
   - ☐ b. the mixture freezes evenly.
   - ☐ c. the ice crystals are broken up.

9. It might take hours to make ice cream if you
   - ☐ a. use your regular freezer instead of a machine.
   - ☐ b. add more salt to the mixture.
   - ☐ c. don't stir often enough.

10. Children can make ice cream because
    - ☐ a. the machines have very simple instructions.
    - ☐ b. the machines have no electrical parts.
    - ☐ c. there are few ingredients and few steps in the process.

Answer Key

Progress Graph

Pacing Graph

Answer Key

1	1. b	2. c	3. a	4. c	5. b	6. a	7. c	8. c	9. b	10. a
2	1. a	2. b	3. b	4. c	5. a	6. a	7. b	8. a	9. a	10. c
3	1. a	2. b	3. b	4. c	5. b	6. c	7. b	8. b	9. a	10. c
4	1. b	2. a	3. b	4. c	5. a	6. b	7. b	8. b	9. a	10. b
5	1. b	2. c	3. b	4. b	5. a	6. b	7. c	8. b	9. c	10. a
6	1. a	2. c	3. a	4. c	5. b	6. a	7. c	8. a	9. a	10. b
7	1. c	2. c	3. b	4. c	5. c	6. a	7. a	8. b	9. a	10. a
8	1. a	2. a	3. c	4. b	5. c	6. b	7. a	8. a	9. c	10. c
9	1. c	2. b	3. c	4. a	5. b	6. c	7. a	8. c	9. c	10. b
10	1. b	2. a	3. b	4. d	5. a	6. b	7. b	8. a	9. b	10. a
11	1. b	2. a	3. b	4. c	5. c	6. c	7. b	8. b	9. b	10. a
12	1. b	2. a	3. c	4. b	5. a	6. a	7. c	8. a	9. c	10. b
13	1. b	2. a	3. c	4. c	5. b	6. a	7. c	8. b	9. a	10. c
14	1. b	2. b	3. c	4. a	5. c	6. b	7. a	8. b	9. a	10. b
15	1. b	2. a	3. b	4. a	5. c	6. a	7. b	8. b	9. c	10. b
16	1. c	2. a	3. b	4. b	5. b	6. c	7. c	8. a	9. a	10. c
17	1. c	2. a	3. a	4. b	5. c	6. b	7. c	8. a	9. b	10. c
18	1. c	2. a	3. c	4. a	5. b	6. b	7. a	8. b	9. a	10. b
19	1. a	2. c	3. c	4. a	5. b	6. a	7. b	8. c	9. a	10. a
20	1. c	2. a	3. a	4. b	5. b	6. b	7. b	8. c	9. a	10. b
21	1. b	2. a	3. a	4. a	5. c	6. a	7. a	8. a	9. a	10. a
22	1. a	2. c	3. a	4. a	5. c	6. b	7. b	8. b	9. b	10. b
23	1. a	2. a	3. c	4. b	5. c	6. a	7. a	8. c	9. b	10. a
24	1. b	2. c	3. b	4. c	5. c	6. c	7. b	8. c	9. b	10. c
25	1. b	2. a	3. c	4. a	5. b	6. c	7. a	8. c	9. a	10. b

26	1. c	2. b	3. b	4. c	5. c	6. a	7. a	8. b	9. a	10. c
27	1. c	2. b	3. b	4. a	5. b	6. a	7. c	8. b	9. c	10. a
28	1. b	2. c	3. a	4. a	5. c	6. b	7. c	8. b	9. a	10. a
29	1. b	2. a	3. b	4. c	5. a	6. b	7. a	8. c	9. b	10. a
30	1. c	2. b	3. b	4. c	5. c	6. a	7. c	8. c	9. c	10. a
31	1. a	2. c	3. a	4. b	5. b	6. b	7. c	8. b	9. b	10. b
32	1. c	2. b	3. c	4. c	5. c	6. b	7. c	8. b	9. c	10. a
33	1. a	2. b	3. c	4. a	5. b	6. b	7. a	8. b	9. b	10. c
34	1. b	2. c	3. a	4. a	5. c	6. b	7. c	8. b	9. c	10. a
35	1. c	2. a	3. a	4. c	5. c	6. b	7. b	8. a	9. b	10. c
36	1. b	2. a	3. c	4. c	5. a	6. b	7. c	8. b	9. c	10. b
37	1. b	2. a	3. c	4. a	5. c	6. c	7. b	8. c	9. b	10. a
38	1. b	2. a	3. a	4. b	5. c	6. c	7. b	8. c	9. a	10. c
39	1. b	2. a	3. a	4. b	5. b	6. a	7. b	8. a	9. a	10. c
40	1. a	2. a	3. c	4. a	5. a	6. a	7. a	8. b	9. b	10. b
41	1. a	2. c	3. b	4. a	5. a	6. a	7. a	8. a	9. c	10. c
42	1. b	2. c	3. b	4. b	5. c	6. a	7. c	8. b	9. a	10. a
43	1. c	2. b	3. c	4. c	5. c	6. a	7. a	8. c	9. c	10. a
44	1. a	2. a	3. c	4. b	5. b	6. b	7. b	8. c	9. a	10. a
45	1. c	2. a	3. c	4. c	5. b	6. b	7. c	8. c	9. c	10. b
46	1. b	2. a	3. a	4. a	5. b	6. a	7. a	8. b	9. c	10. a
47	1. c	2. b	3. c	4. b	5. c	6. a	7. a	8. a	9. c	10. a
48	1. a	2. a	3. a	4. b	5. b	6. b	7. a	8. a	9. c	10. c
49	1. b	2. c	3. a	4. c	5. b	6. b	7. c	8. b	9. b	10. c
50	1. c	2. c	3. a	4. c	5. b	6. c	7. a	8. c	9. a	10. c

Progress Graph (1–25)

Directions: Write your comprehension score in the box under the selection number. Then put an x on the line above each box to show your reading time and words-per-minute reading rate.

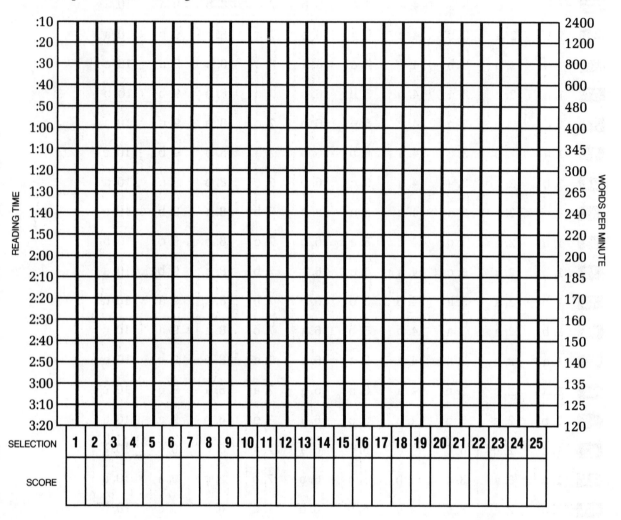

READING TIME		WORDS PER MINUTE
:10		2400
:20		1200
:30		800
:40		600
:50		480
1:00		400
1:10		345
1:20		300
1:30		265
1:40		240
1:50		220
2:00		200
2:10		185
2:20		170
2:30		160
2:40		150
2:50		140
3:00		135
3:10		125
3:20		120

SELECTION: 1 2 3 4 5 6 7 8 9 10 11 12 13 14 15 16 17 18 19 20 21 22 23 24 25

SCORE

Progress Graph (26–50)

Directions: Write your comprehension score in the box under the selection number. Then put an x on the line above each box to show your reading time and words-per-minute reading rate.

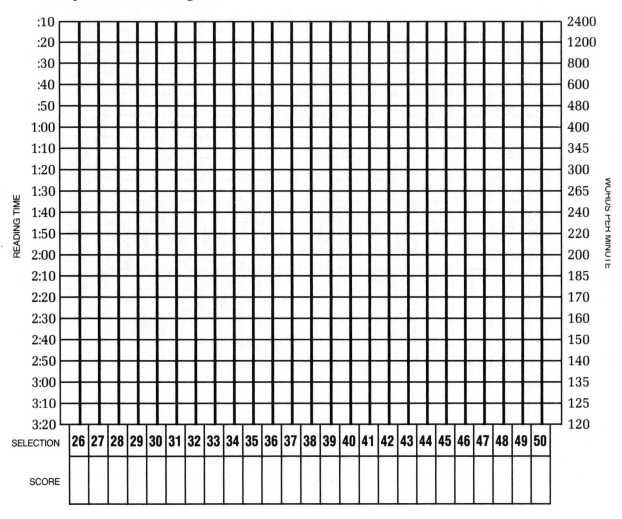

Pacing Graph

Directions: In the boxes labeled "Pace" along the bottom of the graph, write your words-per-minute rate. On the vertical line above each box, put an x to indicate your comprehension score.

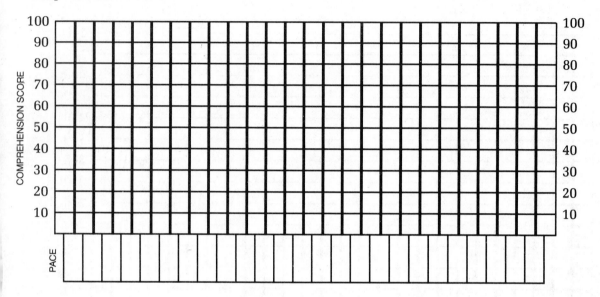